Dimensional Promotions

by David E. Carter

Book Design
Suzanna M.W.

Dimensional Promotions
First published in 2000 by HBI,
an imprint of HarperCollins Publishers
10 East 53rd Street
New York, NY 10022-5299

Hardcover ISBN: 0688-16930-9
Paperback ISBN: 08230-6615-0

Distributed in the U.S. and Canada by
Watson-Guptill Publications
1515 Broadway
New York, NY 10036
Tel: (800) 451-1741
           (732) 363-4511 in NJ, AK, HI
Fax: (732) 363-0338

Distributed throughout the rest of the world by
HBI, an imprint of HarperCollins Publishers
10 East 53rd Street
New York, NY 10022-5299
Fax: (212) 261-6795

2

Printed in Hong Kong by Everbest Printing Company through
Four Colour Imports, Louisville, Kentucky.

Photo credits: The Kaiser Foil record sleeve and Sunsweet coat
pin photos on pages 6 and 7, respectively, were taken by Donavan
Freberg.

Dimensional Promotions

by David E. Carter

If you're asking "what's the logo book guy doing putting out a book on dimensional promotions?" this intro is just for you. And even if you didn't ask the question, you may still find this part interesting. So, read on.

I certainly didn't invent dimensional promotions. Most likely, the father of the "kit" concept was Stan Freberg (see pages 5 - 7).

In 1968, however, I started an advertising agency and my first big client gave me a free rein and (almost) a blank check. My very first campaign for them was a ground-breaking promotion that was written up by *Advertising Age*. (I was 25 at the time, and assumed *everyone* had their first big campaign written up in the major ad trade publication.) I kept producing "kit mailings" for Kentucky Electric Steel, and before long, my little agency was getting calls from clients all over America who wanted me to "do one of your kits for us." We did dimensional promotions for clients literally from Anchorage to Miami, and for clients such as AT&T and DuPont. (And, we did this from Ashland, Kentucky, not exactly a major advertising center.)

Kentucky Electric Steel became one of the best

*In 1970, I created a board game called "The Steel Buying Game" for Kentucky Electric Steel. It sold a **lot** of steel.*

known steel marketers in America—and a lot of this was due to my unusual mail pieces. At a time when "cutting-edge" industrial direct mail meant using a color logo (instead of black only) on a catalog sheet, I was creating "kits" which were the talk of the steel industry. A few of the promotions my agency produced in the 1960s, 70s and early 1980s are shown here and on the next page. I do this for a couple of reasons. One is to show that I did have a creative life before I started the logo books in 1972, and I have a pretty sound background to bring to this book on the topic. Second, I want to set a historic perspective in which the concept of dimensional promotions began its evolution.

Back to the late 1960s. All the major trade magazines did features on my offbeat industrial

promotions. At the time, I didn't know that I was doing anything that unusual. I was simply trying to imitate the creative work of my hero, Stan Freberg. What Freberg had become to TV and radio commercials, I wanted to be to "kit promotions."

Even today, kits—I now call them "dimensional promotions"—are not common. First of all, they are pretty expensive. The typical kits I produced back in the 1970s cost about $15 each. A few of them went for well over $30 per prospect. You can't do that with a mass audience, so kits are most often used to reach a highly select group of prospects. But my clients were mostly industrial advertisers who sold "big ticket" items, so spending $15 each to reach 1,500 or 2,000 prospects was a pretty good investment—especially when some of them produced well over a million dollars in sales. My best kit mailing produced more than $5 million in sales. Not bad.

Another reason why few "kits" are done today is that they are not especially profitable for the creative firm. The big money is in producing big-budget commercials that reach millions of people. Why propose a program that reaches only a few

3

In 1971, I created a comic book character called Steelman, *and we sent to steel buyers boxes which included a t-shirt, "magic" hard hat, and other items. Sales went out the roof.*

In the early 1980s, I began producing a kit to tie in with the Kentucky Derby each year. Customers began to anticipate their annual kit which arrived in late April every year. This "Derby Day Fun Kit" from 1982 got a huge response.

hundred, or at most a few thousand, people? I personally believe that a targeted dimensional promotion can have major impact on the bottom line of an advertiser—especially the small company trying to get recognition from a select group of executives.

Recently, my two daughters (both adults who also work in the advertising/marketing world) saw some of my kits from about 20 years ago. They were surprised how well the quality of work had held up over the years. Then, one of them asked a question: "Was anyone else doing kits back then?"

I honestly didn't know the answer to the question, so I got out the New York Art Directors Annuals from 1969—the year in which I was getting so much publicity for the work I was doing with advertising "kits."

The result: there were exactly **zero** "kit" promotions included in the 1969 book. It was not until many years later that there

was an actual category in the NYADC competition that actually recognized this type promo.

In the 30 years since I produced my first cutting-edge dimensional promotions, there has been a small but growing trend toward firms using kits. For the most part, they are still the province of small companies with a highly targeted prospect list.

As far as I can tell, this is the first book ever produced on the subject of dimensional promotions. For the innovative firm, kit mailings are a way to create strong brand identity to a very narrow target audience on a limited budget. Today, in a time

One year, we sent steel buyers a folding chair. "We want you to have the best seat in the house for the Derby this year" the accompanying booklet read. "So, place this in front of the TV set and watch the race…and while you do it, think of Kentucky Electric Steel." the copy continued. The promotion was sent to about 1,000 steel buyers, at a cost of about $40,000. One recipient commented "you can't throw away a chair."

where media mega-budgets are often needed to make market impact, smaller companies can make a huge splash with a creative kit promotion.

The promotions shown in this book represent some of the most innovative work being produced today. I believe the reader will get a lot of ideas from the creative work found in these pages. And, I applaud all the people who produced the great work and shared it with the readers of this book.

An overdue tribute to Stan Freberg

Without Stan Freberg, this book would never have happened, for a couple of reasons.

If you are familiar with Freberg, you already know one of the reasons. If you don't know just who Stan Freberg is, this is your chance to fill in a gap in your knowledge under the category of "people who changed advertising in a big way."

Just for starters, *Advertising Age* called Stan Freberg "Father of the Funny Commercial."

But this is a book about dimensional promotions, so what is a tribute to Freberg doing here?

As it turns out, Freberg may well be the father of dimensional promotions as well. We'll get to that in a page or so. But first, for the unenlightened, let's answer the question "Who is Stan Freberg?"

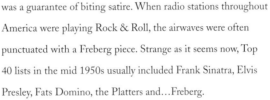

In the early 1950s, Stan Freberg had a number of hit records— most of them satires on *other* hit records. He did takeoffs on songs such as *The Yellow Rose of Texas, The Great Pretender, Heartbreak Hotel* and many others. His satire on the TV show *Dragnet*—titled *St. George and the Dragonet*—was the number one record in America for a time. And his groundbreaking album *Stan Freberg Presents the United States of America* (from the early 1960s) is still so popular that celebrities such as actors Tyne Daily, John Goodman, and Tom Hanks will quote lines from the work when meeting Freberg for the first time.

Freberg contributed so many satirical recordings that he still remains a major icon of American pop culture of the late 20th century. By the time Stan was 26, he had established himself as one of the brightest and funniest men in America. His name on a record was a guarantee of biting satire. When radio stations throughout America were playing Rock & Roll, the airwaves were often punctuated with a Freberg piece. Strange as it seems now, Top 40 lists in the mid 1950s usually included Frank Sinatra, Elvis Presley, Fats Domino, the Platters and…Freberg.

It was in that time period that I was in junior high school, and people first asked me "what are you going to be when you grow up?" (I didn't know. I had always assumed that I would wind up playing shortstop for the New York Yankees.) Freberg was my first role model, although I had never heard the term used at the time. I loved his records, especially *St. George and the Dragonet*. (I can still quote lines from it today.) So when people asked me what I wanted to be when I grew up, I said "I want to be a writer." I didn't tell them I wanted to write like Freberg. (I imagine they heard *writer* and thought *F. Scott Fitzgerald*.)

When I wrote, I often tried to create funny stuff like Freberg. When I was a sophomore in high school, I wrote a creative piece and sent it to a local radio station. The disk jockey, a local legend named Budd Gumm, read it several times on the air, and mentioned my name each time. I was hooked.

While I was practicing my writing skills every evening (instead of doing homework), Freberg was making a huge career move.

In 1956, he created his first advertising campaign. That event was to change his life. Advertising history was also about to be changed. To put Freberg's advertising work into context, you need to understand just how dull most ads were **BS** (Before Stan). Today, we're accustomed to reading a headline, or watching a commercial and *smiling* at a punch line. Maybe even *laughing*. But in the pre-Freberg era, ads *had* no punch line and were mostly excruciatingly dull.

To get some idea of how bland ads were then, I went to the New York Art Directors 1956 Annual of Advertising and checked every page. The nearest thing resembling humor was this print ad for Sunsweet Prunes: A (cartoon) man is shown

Stan Freberg, circa 1958

with a tuba; the headline says "Sunsweet in the morning keeps me in tune all day." That was the funniest headline in the whole book. Seriously. (Ironically, Sunsweet became a major Freberg client a few years later.)

Freberg's ad campaigns got consumer attention, because they were so different (no one else was doing funny advertising then) but they also got free media exposure, for the same reason. In a campaign for Pacific Air Lines (now merged into US Airways),

5

he directly addressed the fearful flyer with this headline: "Hey there! You with the sweat in your palms." Even Freberg's media strategies were offbeat. He placed that ad as a full page in the *New York Times*. The airline executives seriously questioned this move, since the airline didn't even fly to New York. "Trust me," Stan said. When David Brinkley held up the ad on the NBC Nightly News, they never questioned him again. It was common for a mid-budget Freberg campaign to get millions of dollars in free publicity, because *nobody* was doing ads anything like Stan's.

In the late 1950s, Freberg created a still-famous ad campaign for Kaiser Foil. At that time, Reynolds Wrap was the dominant aluminum foil brand, and Henry J. Kaiser had a plan to make a dent in their market share. Freberg was called in to handle the ads.

The campaign was on both radio and television, and featured a "soap opera" format. The spots opened with organ music in the background; the narrator opened with "Kaiser Aluminum Foil Salesman Faces Life…" The spots had Smathers going home after "another in a series of unsuccessful days" trying to get grocers to stock Kaiser Foil. Smathers often had to explain to his daughter that "the mean old grocers won't stock Kaiser Foil."

Freberg's distinctive voice, already well known from his records, was the voice of Smathers. In the animated TV commercials, our hero would walk into a grocery store and say "Clark Smathers, Kaiser Aluminum Foil…"

The grocer would say "we won't need any, we don't have any room on our shelves…"

Smathers, outraged, would say "What? No room on the shelf…" The animated Smathers would then shove the other foil out of the way. Smathers would say, "*No room on the shelf?* This is America. There's room for every man. Big man, little man, other foil, Kaiser Foil, that's the American way."

As Freberg's voice expressed his indignation, the animated Smathers opens his brief case; little animated soldiers are marching around back and forth, a little flag goes up, and a skyrocket goes off. Then Smathers says to the grocer "you know what I'm going to do—I'm going to make some animated TV commercials, put them on TV and tell people the truth about your not stocking Kaiser Foil." The grocer says, "he wouldn't do that—would he?" Smathers hits the guy on the head with a mallet (WHAM!) and says "not if you'd stock a little Kaiser Foil."

The First Dimensional Promotion

Freberg planned and produced a "kit"—which was distributed to thousands of retail grocers around the country. The box included a medal that grocers could pin on; it said "DON'T HIT ME; I'VE GOT IT". The strategy would be that shoppers would see the medal on the grocer; it would hopefully cause somebody to ask "got what?" And the grocer would say, "Kaiser Foil, aisle 17."

The kit also included a 45 rpm record in a purple, black, and yellow dust cover; everything was color keyed (with purple and

45 rpm record from the Kaiser Foil kit

black and yellow), and the medal was the same colors. Finally, there was a small cardboard mallet the grocer could use to fight off the overzealous Kaiser salesman.

Freberg recalls the campaign well. "I wanted to have the medals printed on aluminum foil. They said 'we can't make it out of foil; we're going to make it out of cardboard.' I said 'why not' and they said 'foil is too expensive.' I said 'you've got warehouses full of it. If there's anything you've got a lot of, it's Kaiser Aluminum Foil.'

"In the end, they were made from cardboard. They also gave the grocer a purple first aid kit with band aids in case the Kaiser Foil salesman hit him with the mallet. We let the grocers in on the campaign ahead of time, and he thought 'I don't want to be a bad guy, and they'll give me that medal I can pin on.' Before this, Kaiser couldn't get any new placements of Kaiser Foil. When this campaign got 11,000 new placements (new retail outlets), *Newsweek* did a story. The campaign eventually opened up 43,000 new placements.

"The account executive of Young & Rubicam, a graduate of Harvard Business School, kept reminding me about his education. He'd say things like 'If you had gone to *the school*, you would understand that advertising can *never* force distribution.' He kept telling me that over and over: *advertising can't force distribution.*

"After the 43,000 new placements of foil. I said to this guy— 'well, it worked out all right, didn't it? I thought you said advertising can't force distribution.' He said, 'It *can't.* Something must have gone wrong.'

"Edgar Kaiser, one of the sons of Henry Kaiser, said his father almost had a heart attack when he first saw the animated salesman walk in on a commercial in the Maverick show and say 'Clark Smathers, Kaiser Aluminum Foil,' and the grocer says 'what can I do for you' and Smathers hits the grocer over the head (WHAM) and says 'you can stock a little Kaiser Foil for a change, that's what you can do.' He literally almost had a coronary. After the campaign was over, his son said, 'well, Dad, that worked out all right didn't it?' The father said, 'yes I admit it did.' His son, Ed, said 'now do you still hate Freberg?' His father said 'it isn't that I hate Freberg, I just hate hitting grocers over the head.'

"Edgar Kaiser himself told me that story in San Francisco when I met him later at a reception."

Another Freberg Dimensional Promotion

Another wildly successful Freberg campaign (400% increase in sales) was for Sunsweet Prunes. Freberg was forced to include a coupon in print ads, and the result was an (unplanned) dimensional promotion sent to selected customers.

Freberg describes the event: "At one point, I was doing a newspaper campaign for Sunsweet, and they made me put this coupon in. Coupons are a pain in the butt and ruin the graphics layout, but they want it so people can cut it out and bring it in to the grocer. I made the type so small, maybe about a point-and-a-half, the smallest type possible, so you can only read it with a magnifying glass. I had all the legal stuff in, and then I wrote *yadda yadda yadda, all this legal stuff, on and on it goes, like the treaty of Versailles. Who's got the time or patience to read all this stuff? Oh, well I guess we have to say blah, blah, blah.* And the last line said *this coupon printed on the head of a* **pin** *if more convenient.*

"The Sunsweet people never even read it before it ran. All of a sudden, they called me one day from San Jose, and said 'we're getting these strange letters from people, that say "as a matter of fact, it would be more convenient on the head of a pin. Please render me this coupon on the head of a pin." What are they talking about?' I had to confess that I had added a little ad lib in the legal coupon. They said 'That's funny. Now, how do you deal with this?'

"I said, 'Let me call Sarasota, Florida, and see if there's anybody left with Ringling Brothers Side Show who would be about 94-years old, sitting on a porch somewhere fanning themselves, who actually does the Lord's Prayer on the head of a pin.' I tried, but I could not find anybody in America who did that work any more. So, I printed that coupon on a pin—like a pin on a coat—about 3 - 4 inches across.

"All the people who had written in asking about the coupon on the head of a pin received the coat pin, along with a letter that I

The Sunsweet coupon was printed on a "pin"—to be pinned on a coat. Freberg would have preferred to have had it on the head of a real pin.

wrote. Some people wrote back and said 'I'm disappointed, I really wanted it on the head of a pin.'"

Freberg's entry into the world of advertising was done with his typical bite. He often spoofed the agencies who (reluctantly) hired him. His corporate name was (and still is) actually *Freberg, Ltd. (but not very)*. In the 1960s, he formed THYME, Inc., "a division of Parsley, Sage, Rosemary & Osborne." (For the uninitiated, this was a takeoff on the famous ad agency, Batten, Barton, Durstine & Osborne, as well as a spoof on a popular song of the day. (Even on his advertising letterhead, Freberg was still lampooning popular music.) The letterhead had a red border around it. "I didn't want to copy *National Geographic*," Stan said. "So I used red rather than yellow." *Time* magazine didn't see the humor in that.

Many times, clients would hire Freberg over the (often loud) objections of their agencies. Freberg did work that was very un-advertising, and this tended to make account executives a little nervous. Especially when Freberg broke all of the "rules" of advertising and had major marketing successes. For example, he spurned the typical 30- and 60-second radio commercial form, and once produced a 6-1/2 minute spot for Butter-Nut coffee.

His style of advertising was his own; it soon became the blueprint for the "creative revolution" of advertising in the mid-1960s. Indeed, the Golden Age of Advertising might trace its lineage back to Freberg's first ad campaign in 1956 for Contadina Tomato Paste ("Who puts eight great tomatoes in that little bitty can?"). Freberg's first ad campaign was a hit; *Ad Age* chose it as one of the top two marketing successes of the year. Yes, Freberg changed the world of advertising. Along the way, he was a dominant creative force in the industry for a number of years, winning 21 Clio Awards.

And, from my personal point of view, his work in advertising influenced my career choice. In high school, I wanted to write satire like Freberg. By the time I got to college, I was an advertising major, and wanted to write *ads* like Freberg. My early work was often directly imitative (I avoid using the words "rip-off") of Stan's writing.

For most of my professional life, I was slightly bothered that I never did write anything as well as Freberg. Only recently did I realize that *nobody* wrote as well as Stan Freberg. For me, and for others, he set a high standard of excellence that we could only hope to approach, but never equal.

Thanks, Stan. You made a difference.

David Carter

Stan Freberg in the '70s

7

Dimensional Promotions

As my advertising career progressed, I found that my client base was primarily industrial accounts — such as a steel manufacturer. In the 1960s, industrial ads were all dull, and industrial direct mail was synonymous with a black and white catalog sheet of specs and prices set in agate type.

Beginning in 1968, I had an innovative, trusting client who allowed me to use the Freberg approach for direct mail. Before long, my client, Kentucky Electric Steel, had become known for its breakthrough marketing. The dimensional promotions I produced won six major awards from the Direct Marketing Association, including two in the same year. (Only 50 campaigns were honored by DMA each year.) Most of the other campaigns were multi-page letters.

If Freberg was the pioneer of dimensional promotions, I was following the trail he blazed. Along the way, my agency gained a national reputation for our innovative "kits." Only later did I realize that few other firms were doing this at the time.

My personal favorite dimensional promotion is the "Steel Buyer's Idea Kit" I produced in 1978 for Kentucky Electric Steel. If I ever did anything that measured up to the "Freberg standard," this might be it.

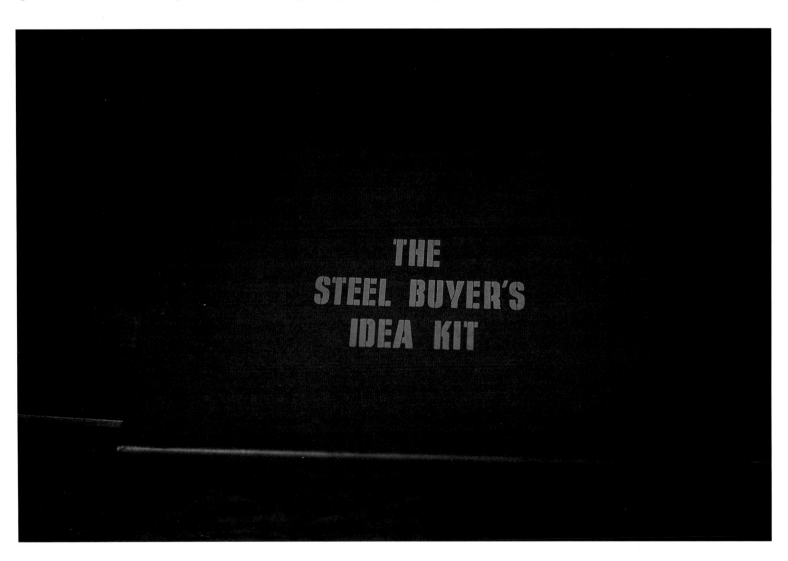

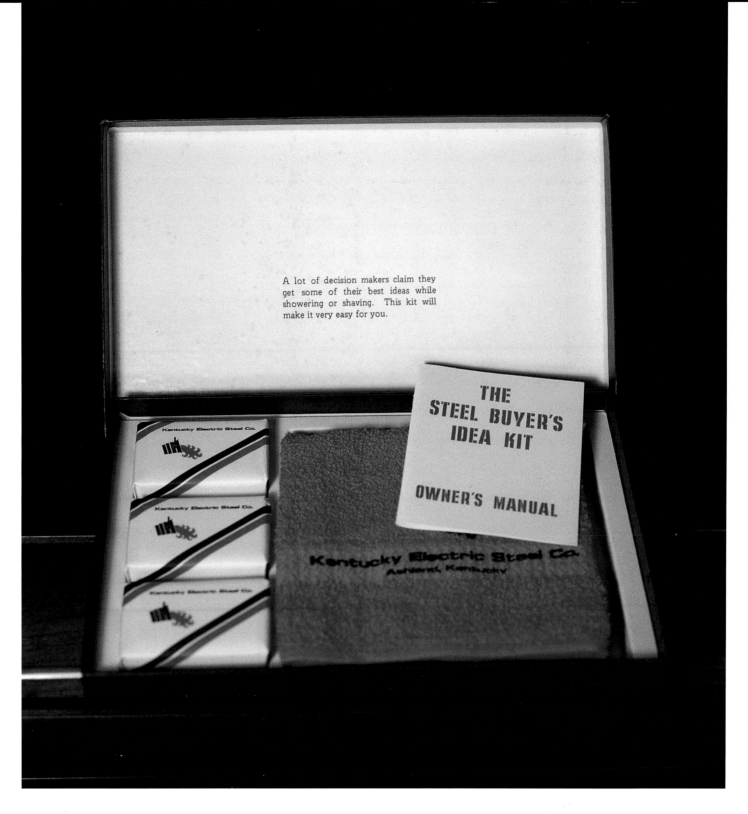

A lot of decision makers claim they get some of their best ideas while showering or shaving. This kit will make it very easy for you.

THE STEEL BUYER'S IDEA KIT

OWNER'S MANUAL

The Steel Buyer's Idea Kit included custom-produced soap as well as imprinted towels. Copy premise was: "many decision makers get some of the best ideas while showering or shaving. This makes it very easy for you."

This piece sold more than $5 million worth of steel; It was so much in demand by customers that 500 extras had to be produced to take care of calls like "I got your kit, but my boss took it. Can I get another one?"

NOTE: This piece won the Clio Award in 1980 under the category of "Industrial/Agricultural Promotions." It is interesting to note that **all** of the other finalists were essentially brochures or catalogs.

"This promotion was designed to gain new clients for a photography studio. Their primary focus was clients in the food industry.

"The studio's marketing director actually hand delivered the pizza box with the promo inside. The marketing director showed up at each location dressed in a pizza delivery outfit and a custom-made pizza warmer container. The marketing director would pull the pizza box out of the warmer and hand it to the client. The box included a coupon in which the intended client could call the photo studio and an actual pizza would be delivered to the client's office or at the photo studio. In either case, the marketing director would have a chance to show the work produced by the studio.

"The client wanted to emphasize service and quality, so the headlines were 'We Really Deliver' and 'Great Images Any Way You Slice It.'"

Creative Firm:
   double entendre inc.
   Seattle, Washington
Client: Conrad & Co.
Business:
   Photographer
Creative:
   double entendre inc.

10

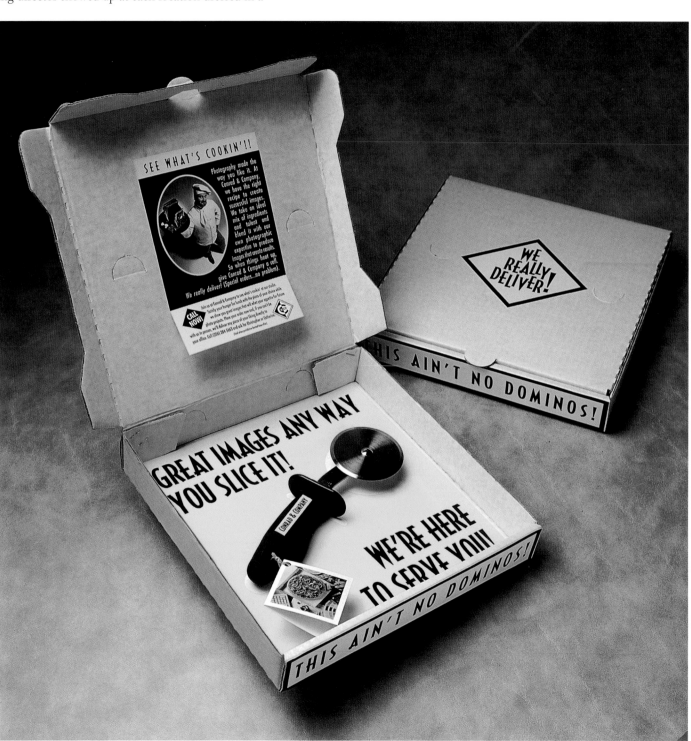

"Each year, The New York Times publishes special issues of its Sunday Magazine, dedicated to one particular topic. For 1999, six special issues were themed to present different aspects of the millennium. The New York Times needed to announce the content and advertising deadlines for these upcoming issues. Clarke/Thompson created a promotion booklet, branding the Millennium Series with visuals highlighting key moments in the past 1,000 years, and custom-designed icons representing each of the special issues.

"As a companion piece to this highly successful promotion, Clarke/Thompson articulated the Millennium Series identity into a Champagne Six-Pack, which was sent to V.I.P. advertisers during the holiday season. Each bottle wore a letterpress-printed hang-tag, featuring the name of a special issue, along with its publication date and deadlines."

Creative Firm:
   Clarke/Thompson Advertising & Design
   New York, New York
Client: The New York Times
Business: Publisher
Art Director: Viviane Tubiana

"This promotion was produced to promote a merger meeting of two of the largest independent providers of kidney dialysis services, TRC and RTC. The meeting was planned for Caesar's Palace, and the visual theme of the piece focused on the architectural references to a roman column.

"Creating an 'inviting' introduction to the merger meeting, the column invitation was meant to raise the enthusiasm and curiosity of the employees— enticing them to attend an otherwise mundane event. The boxes were mailed out individually, with mailing labels on the grey interior wrap. When the wrap was removed and the box opened, a corrugated column was revealed. All of the event paperwork (itinerary, map, enrollment, etc.) was rolled into this column."

Creative Firm: IE Design
  Studio City, California
Client: Total Renal Care
Business: Health care
Creative: Marcie Carson

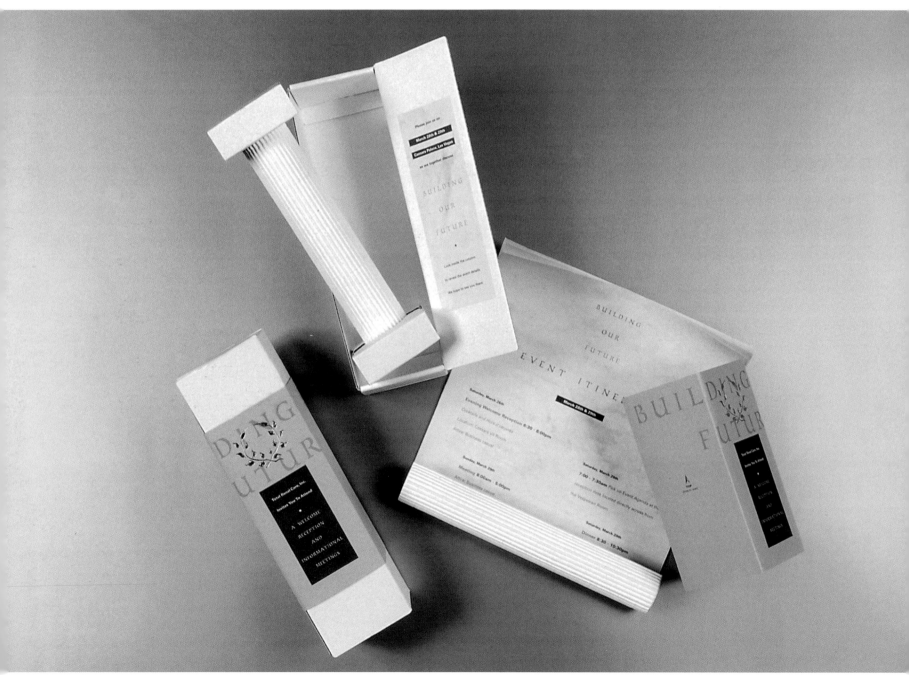

13

"This mailer, sent out at Christmas time, promoted the design company—Tor Petterson & Partners.

"The company's symbol is a camel walking through the eye of a needle, symbolizing that one can visually achieve the impossible."

Creative Firm: Tor Pettersen & Partners
London, England
Client: Tor Pettersen & Partners
Business: Design firm
Creative: Tor Pettersen,
Nick Kendall, Claire Barnett

"This dimensional piece is birthday greetings sent to actors, directors, producers, etc., involved in the movies being managed by Turner Entertainment.

"The birthday cake is spring loaded with a rubber band and snaps into shape when it is pulled out of its envelope."

Creative Firm: Sabingrafik, Inc.
  Carlsbad, California
Client: Turner Entertainment
Business: Film library/archive
Art Directors: Alison Hill, Joe Swaney
Illustrator: Tracy Sabin

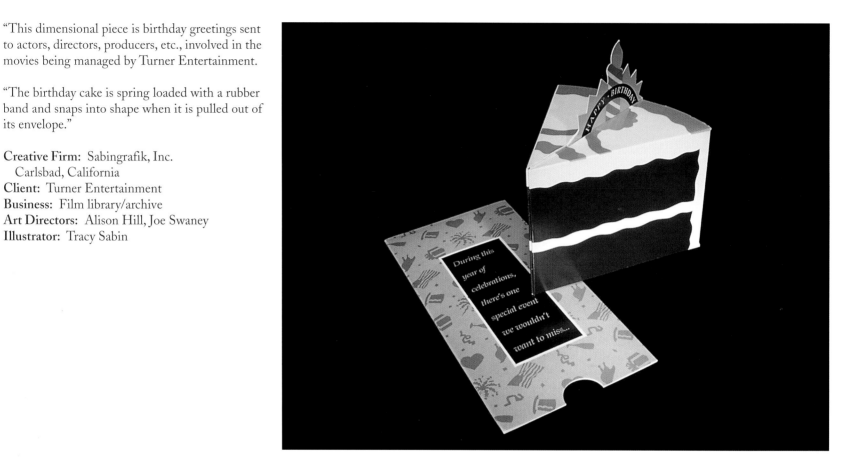

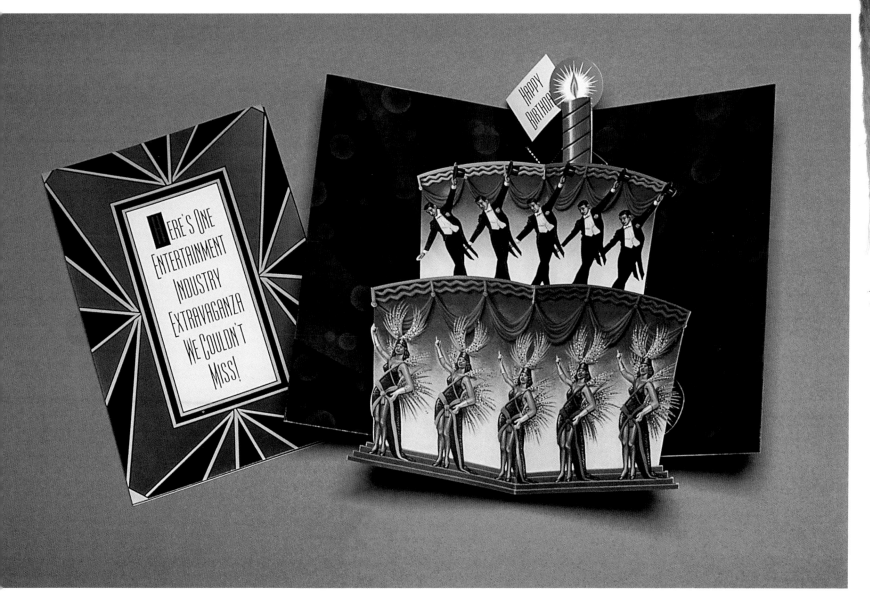

"Taylor Made Golf Company needed to separate and emphasize their new products and technology from their existing products. Since all their products have one main catalogue, the solution became an interactive piece which allowed golf shop operators to touch and feel the new products and to stimulate dialogue at the first touch. Follow-up literature reiterated points and facts."

Creative Firm:
   Laura Coe Design Associates
   San Diego, California
Client: Taylor Made Golf Co., Inc.
Business: Golf product company
Art Director: Laura Coe Wright

16

"The heavy-duty corrugated Nubbins book was designed as a marketing tool for the Taylor Made sales force. The sleek outside of the box simply read 'nubbins,' with an embossed textured label to touch and pique the interest of the recipient.

"When the box was opened, it revealed a similar embossed texture on the Nubbins' putter face. Foam inserts held Taylor Made's new putter along with two competitors' putters and three balls. The key account shops were not only able to read and learn about the new putter technology, but also put it to the test by actually testing Nubbins with their competition!"

Creative Firm: Laura Coe Design Associates
    San Diego, California
Client: Taylor Made Golf Co., Inc.
Business: Golf product company
Creative: Laura Coe Wright, Leanne Leveillee

"This is a birth announcement for my third child, who also happened to be my third daughter. It was also shamelessly used to promote my graphic design consulting business.

"The piece is die cut and scored to fold into a cube—a child's building block. It was folded and mailed flat in an envelope, requiring assembly upon receipt (like many children's toys). As the flat piece is opened, the copy, in sequence, paraphrases a popular child's nursery rhyme, '1 little 2 little, 3 little Glasers...Three Little Glaser Girls. Nicole and Kelsey [the older daughters] are thrilled to announce the arrival of their new baby sister...' The color scheme is pink with 'baby blue' accents. The numbers on the sides are large, like numbers on a child's set of blocks, while the top and bottom of the cube feature stylized illustrations of a teddy bear and a rocking horse."

Creative Firm: Wet Paper Bag Graphic Design
　　Fort Worth, Texas
Client: Bonita Glaser
Business: Mother
Creative People: Lewis Glaser, Bonita Glaser

18

We made a bundle this year, and we'd like to share it with all our friends!

Scott & Karina announce the birth of their daughter
Kaiya Antolin Brown
Born October 15, 1998 weighing 8 lbs., 2 oz.

19

"To announce the birth of their first child in a creative, dimensional way, this humorous mailing was devised."

Creative Firm: Jack Nadel, Inc.
  Los Angeles, California
Client: Scott Brown
Business: Personal
Art Director, Illustrator: Scott Brown

"Designed for Titleist Golf Company, the Demo Days Promotion launched the introduction of new golf clubs. Sent to golf stores, the kit included a poster, video and brochure. Designed to be viewed as a family of informational pieces, the vibrant colors attracted customers to read and understand the new technology and invite them to give the club a swing."

Creative Firm: Laura Coe Design Associates
    San Diego, California
Client: Titleist Golf Company
Business: Golf products company
Creative People: Lauren Bruhn, Darryl Glass

20

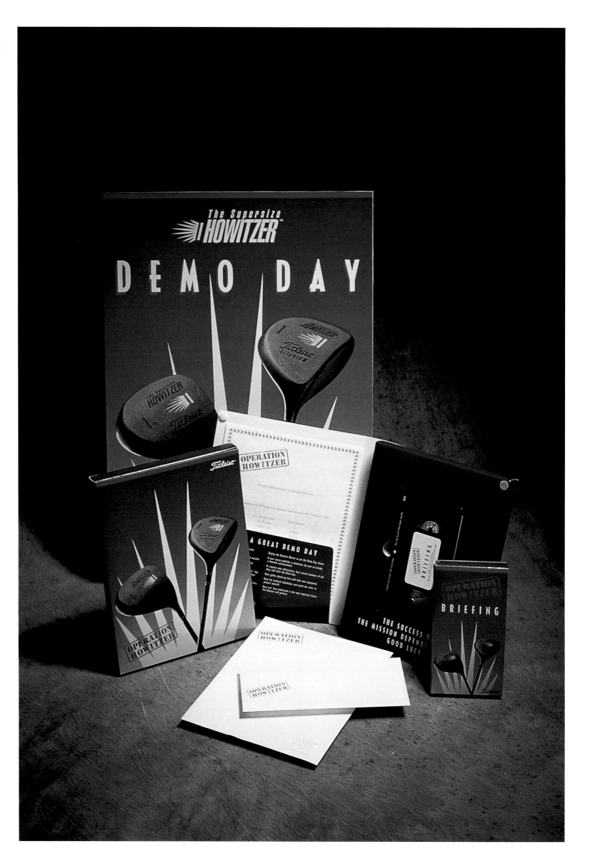

Editor's Note: *This is not your traditional promotion. However, it is so striking that I decided it should go into this book. After all, it is dimensional, and it could be construed as "being sent" to a select group of people.*

Without question, the splash pattern on the jet, referred to as "road kill" makes a dynamic impression when the Herman Miller jet arrives.

Creative Firm: BBK Studio
Grand Rapids, Michigan
Client: Herman Miller
Business: Furniture manufacturer
Creative: Michael Barile

Wear this button to our annual meeting
and celebrate a great year and our birthday.

I ♥ MLHR

A great year, a great history, a great future.
1998 Annual Report   Herman Miller, Inc., and Subsidiaries

HAPPY 75TH BIRTHDAY
HERMAN MILLER!

"The 1998 Herman Miller annual report is very
much unlike the typical financial document. Its
dimensional cover even features a cluster of 'star'
confetti. Inside, various pages feature a pop-up
smiley face, a balloon, a button, a paper hat that
you can make, and a pop-out megaphone."

Creative Firm: BBK Studio
  Grand Rapids, Michigan
Client: Herman Miller
Business: Furniture manufacturer
Creative: Yang Kim, Steve Frykholm,
  Clark Malcolm, Lake County Press

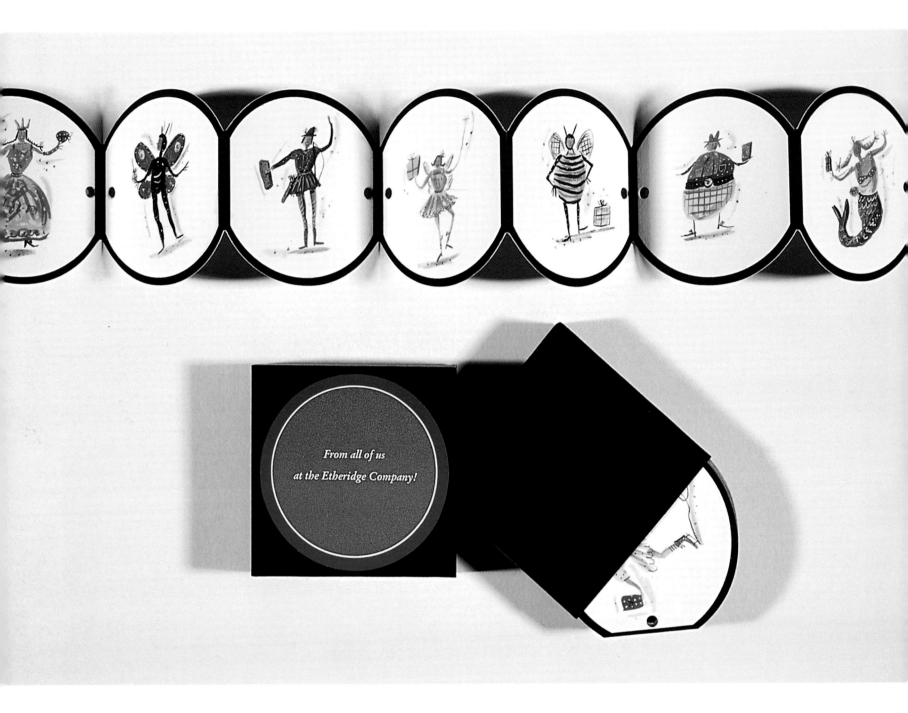

From all of us
at the Etheridge Company!

"The Ethridge Company, a printer with the ability
to do intricate hand assembly of printed items, has
a holiday card series."

Creative firm: BBK Studio
  Grand Rapids, Michigan
Client: The Etheridge Company
Business: Printer
Creative: Yang Kim

"Tucked away in a teak wood box is a book on the *Chronicles of the America's Cup*. A story told of the spectacular competition is evident in vivid color photos and intricately varnished maps of courses sailed. Mailed to the heads of Fortune 500 companies, its intent was to lure them into a monetary donation. This promotion included the coffee-table style book, a poster and video. The promotion was a success, meeting the intended goal set by our client, Dennis Conner Sports."

Creative Firm: Laura Coe Design Associates
    San Diego, California
Client: Dennis Conner Sports
Business: Yacht racing
Creative: Laura Coe Wright, Lauren Bruhn

Editor's note (again): *You probably didn't expect to find a letterhead design in this book, either, but this piece serves as a dimensional promotion every time the business sends it out.*

"This is a letterhead and business card for a fiber artist. She creates weavings using all manner of cloth, natural fiber and handmade paper. She needed stationery for business correspondence, as well as a way to promote her business of creating and selling her craft.

"An elaborate direct mail piece was not economically feasible, because of the highly specialized, and limited nature, of the audience for her work. Therefore, we decided to make the letterhead system as interesting and unusual as possible, so it could double as a business promotion.

"The designer selected a rayon-fiber paper and did a simple typographic treatment with a slightly feminine quality to reflect the personality and gender of the artist. The unusual, and three-dimensional, part of the package is the variegated metallic thread. Each sheet of letterhead and business cards is run through a sewing machine. This creates a striking contrast to the 'average' flat printed paper letterhead, while visually reinforcing the artist's medium.

"This has been highly successful for the client, and was quite inexpensive to produce."

Creative Firm: Wet Paper Bag Graphic Design
        Fort Worth, Texas
Client: Cranford Creations
Business: Fiber artist
Creative: Lewis Glaser

27

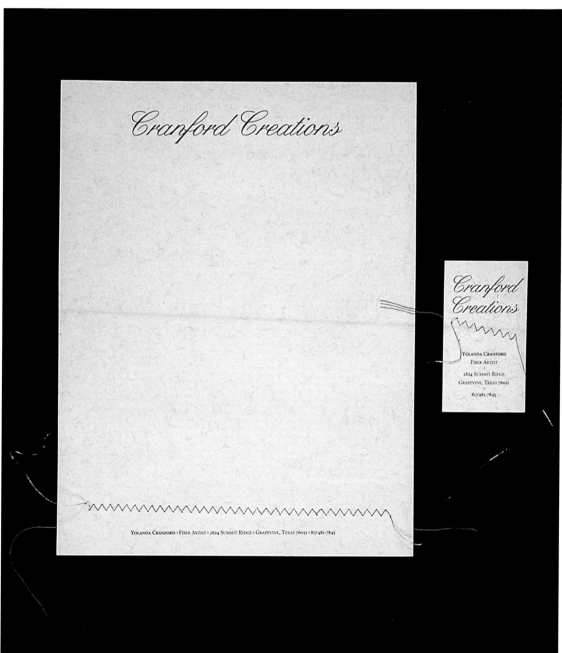

Designer Tracy Sabin took dimensional promotions to the internet with this innovative 20-piece self promotion. The promotion is for "Paperland" and each piece can be downloaded, output on a color printer and assembled. To see the full promotion, including photos of the assembled pieces, go to:
http://tracy.sabin.com/paperland.html

PAPERLAND
PROJECT ONE · THE HERO'S FOUNTAIN · PUZZLE PIECE 1 OF 20 · Paper Land Active Yardwe

Town Center Fountain

❶ Cut out all pieces along their outside edges.

❷ Cut along all slits, including the slit in the pool.

❸ Curve the fountain base into a circle inserting the escutcheons into slits A, B, C and D until you have completed the circle. Insert Tab E into Slit E. Glue the escutcheons down.

❹ Fold and glue the statue halves together and insert Tab F into Slit F in the Cobblestone Base.

❺ Push the statue, from the back, through the slit in the pool. Insert Tabs G through J into Slits G through J in the Cobblestone Base.

Ta Dah!

Cobblestone Base

Statue

Slit G   Slit H

Slit F

Slit J   Slit I

← Escutcheon

← Fountain Base

Tab F

Slit E   Slit A   Slit B   Slit C   Slit D   Tab E

Tab J   Tab I   Tab H   Tab G

Alberto Emilio Gator, R.
Paperland's **Esteemed**
who discovered that
dimensional sheets of pa
be cut, folded and glued
three dimensional wo

©1999

PAPE

❶ Cut out the Town Ha balcony. Be sure to fish all the way to th roofline.

❷ Cut a slit along the Slit B and Slit C.

❸ Fold back the wall s halves together and Slit A.

❹ Insert

Town Hall

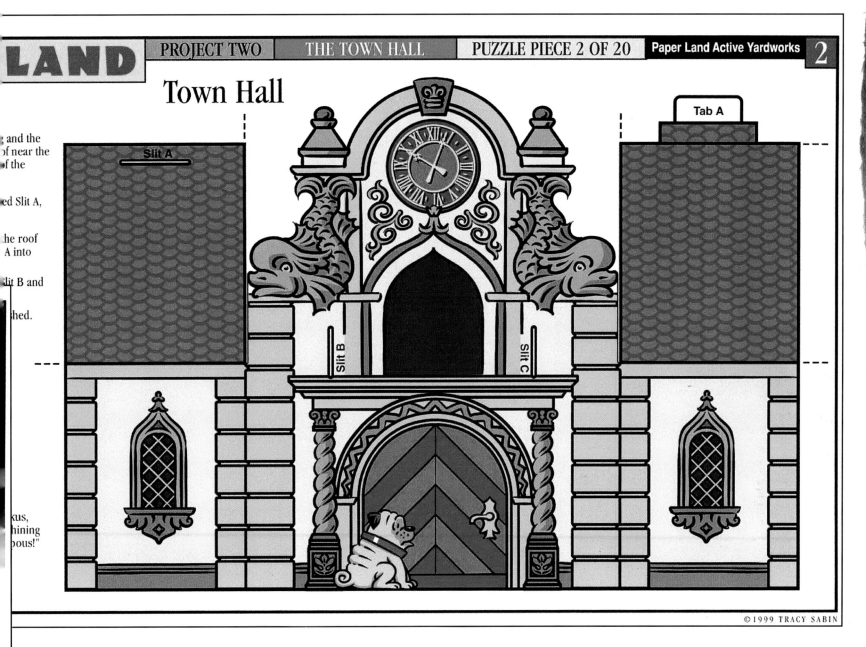

Slit A

Tab A

Slit B

Slit C

and the
of near the
of the

ed Slit A,

he roof
A into

lit B and

hed.

us,
hining
ous!"

29

© 1999 TRACY SABIN

Creative Firm: Sabingrafik, Inc.
Carlsbad, California
Client: Sabingrafik, Inc.
Business: Graphic design/illustration
Creative: Tracy Sabin

1. Cut out all pieces al[...]
   their outside edges.

3. Fold the Roadbed a[...]
   insert Tabs A, B, C a[...]
   A, B, C and D. Glue

4. Insert the Unlabeled[...]
   into slits E, F, G and[...]
   down. Both Bridge S[...]
   be facing the same [...]

5. Insert Tabs I and J i[...]
   Slits I and J.

6. Fold and glue the tw[...]
   halves of the bear[...]

30

Barrel Organ

1. Cut out all pieces along their outside edges.

2. Cut along all slits, including the slits in the cobble-stone base.

3. Cut out the inset organ pipe area on the Organ Facade and cut along the outside edges of the pipes down to the two long perpendicular lines. Fold the pipes back at the base and forward at the dashed line.

4. Fold the sides and striped roof of the Organ Enclosure and insert the curved tabs into slits A through F. Glue the curved tabs down so they cover the lettering.

5. Insert tabs G, H and I into Slits G, H and I in the cobblestone base.

6. Fold over the two sides of the organist and glue them together. Insert Tab J into the unlabeled slit on the cobblestone base.

Voila!

Gertrude Gette Down, **Organist Extraordinaire**, whose talents are much appreciated throughout the township.

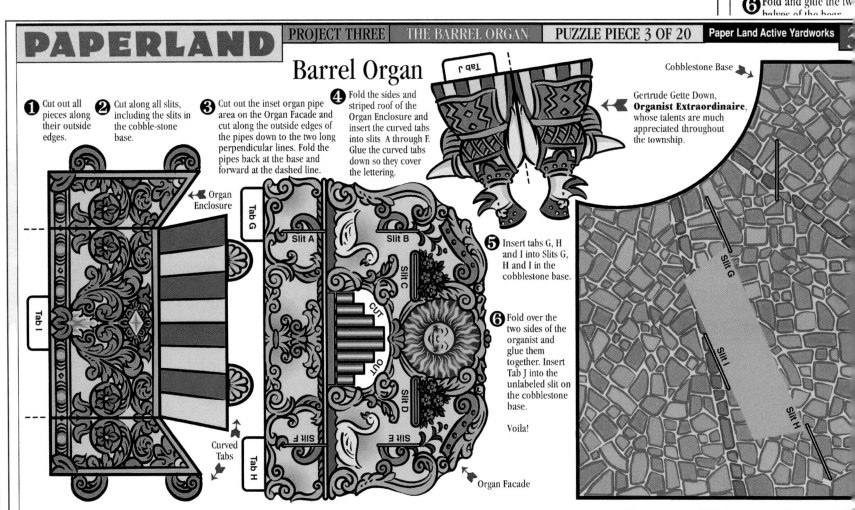

Organ Enclosure

Tab I

Curved Tabs

Tab G

Tab H

Slit A

Slit B

Slit C

Slit D

CUT

OUT

Slit F

Slit E

Organ Facade

Tab J

Cobblestone Base

Slit G

Slit I

Slit H

© 1999 TRACY S[...]

Bridge

Cut along all slits, including the Bear Slit in the Bridge Side.

...d lines and ...lits

Tabs ...em ...d

Bruno Pescatore, **Devoted Bridge Fisherman**. If you feel ambitious, you can tie a piece of thread on the end of a toothpick and stick it in his hand for a fishing pole!

Bear Slit

Bridge Side

Slit F

Slit E

Slit G

Slit H

Slit D

Slit C

Roadbed ➤➤

A B I J C D

◄◄ Unlabeled Roadbed Tabs ➤➤

Slit I

Slit J

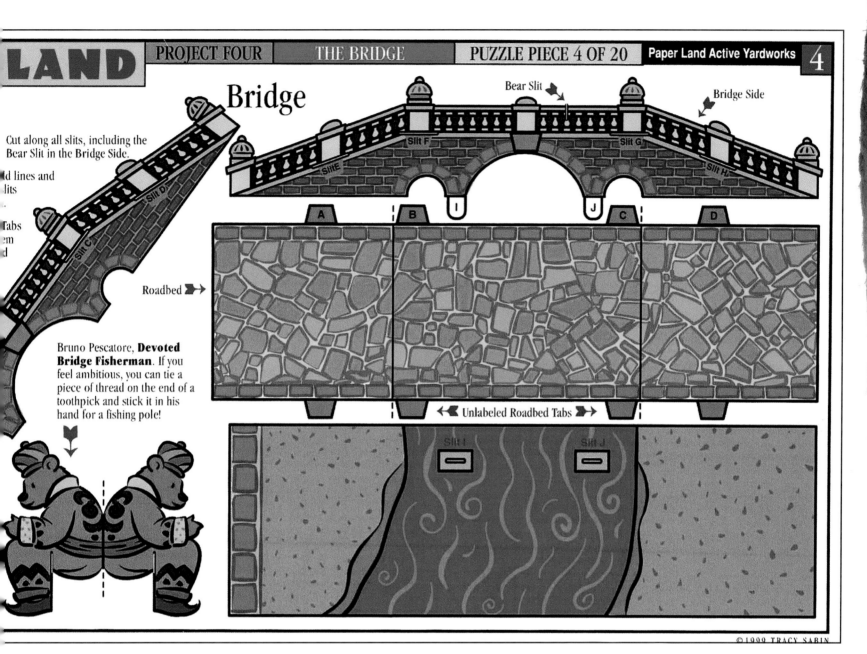

"Everybody needs to get a little frustration out of their system now and then. To promote TCM's boxing movie festival, Hollywood Heavyweight, a custom-printed punching bag was designed to fit the bill. The bag was shipped to cable operators preinflated, in a gigantic box, to guarantee the recipients' attention.

"The design itself was a modern take on city gym fight-night posters of the 30s and 40s, where no-name fighters like Rocky Graziano got their start. The large head of Robert DeNiro was a subtle hint that with a simple copier enlargement of a photo, anybody's head could be substituted. Who knows? Maybe the boss's face might end up on it!"

Creative Firm: Banks Albers Design
   Atlanta, Georgia
Client: Turner Classic Movies
Business: Cable network/entertainment
Creative: Scott Banks, Kevin Fitzgerald

32

"This sales promotion item was created to appeal to the basketball fanatic. The sales rep would use this as a vehicle to deliver game tickets, candy basketballs, or other related items. It worked well because if Gaylord had plants in cities that didn't have a professional team, then they usually had a college team that the customer supported. Gaylord also has a sky box in Chicago and would use this as a self-promotional item.

"The neat catch is that when you open the top, there is a sound bite that plays a standing ovation."

Creative Firm: Gaylord Graphics
    Carol Stream, Illinois
Client: Gaylord Container Corporation
Creative: Jerry Farrell

Coffee mug, ball cap, and t-shirt were all developed to dispel any fear of computer-caused cataclysm by conveying the message, "I'M Y2OK."

Creative Firm: Larsen Design + Interactive
  Minneapolis, Minnesota
Client: Larsen Design + Interactive
Business: Design firm
Creative Director: Tim Larsen
Designer: Sascha Boecker

34

"A marketing goal was set to increase gross sales in fiscal 1998 by 10%, thereby breaking $50 million.

"In order to achieve the goal, a Hawaiian vacation weekend was awarded as an incentive for reaching the $50 million gross sales goal. Additionally, many various motivational items branded with the 'Hawaii 5-0' logo were given away during the year to keep this goal top of mind."

Creative Firm: Jack Nadel, Inc.
  Los Angeles, California
Client: Jack Nadel, Inc.
Business: Promotional advertising
Art Directors, Illustrators: Scott Brown,
  Miguel Rosa

"This yearly event to raise money for Hackensack University Medical Center will be held at Grand Central Terminal in NYC this year. The theme is 'On Track For the Year 2000'. Incorporating three tickets (including directions and parking) in a special envelope, all the information about the event is adhered to the front of the unfolding invitation. The photos are vintage, and printed as sepia tones, with the type for 2000 incorporating the old with the new, looking towards the year 2000."

Creative Firm: John Kneapler Design
    New York, New York
Client: Hackensack University Medical Center
Business: Hospital
Creative: John Kneapler, Colleen Shea

36

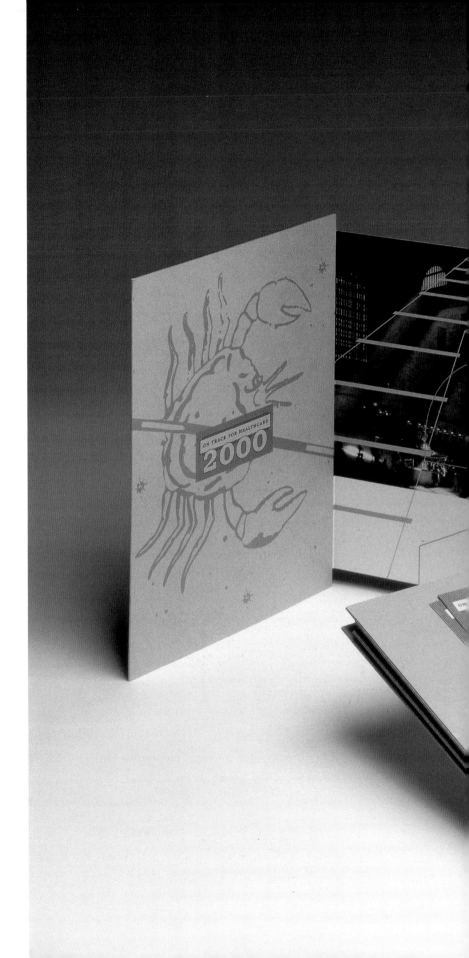

37

"To introduce Salon Selectives to the trade, a unique and memorable presentation was created including an invitation and presentation piece. The Andy Warhol theme was carried across the 'paint can' and the invitation."

Creative Firm: Di Donato Associates
   Chicago, Illinois
Client: Helene Curtis
   (Unilever Home & Personal Care)
Business: HBA
Creative Director: Peter Di Donato
Designer: Marshall Faircloth

"Fruits of Their Labor" invitation is a humorous, if eyebrow-raising, way to get the desired attention for this event.

Creative Firm: M & Co.
    New York, New York
Client: Gay & Lesbian Task Force
Business: Gay organization
Art Director: Stefan Sagmeister
Designers: Stefan Sagmeister,
    Tom Walker

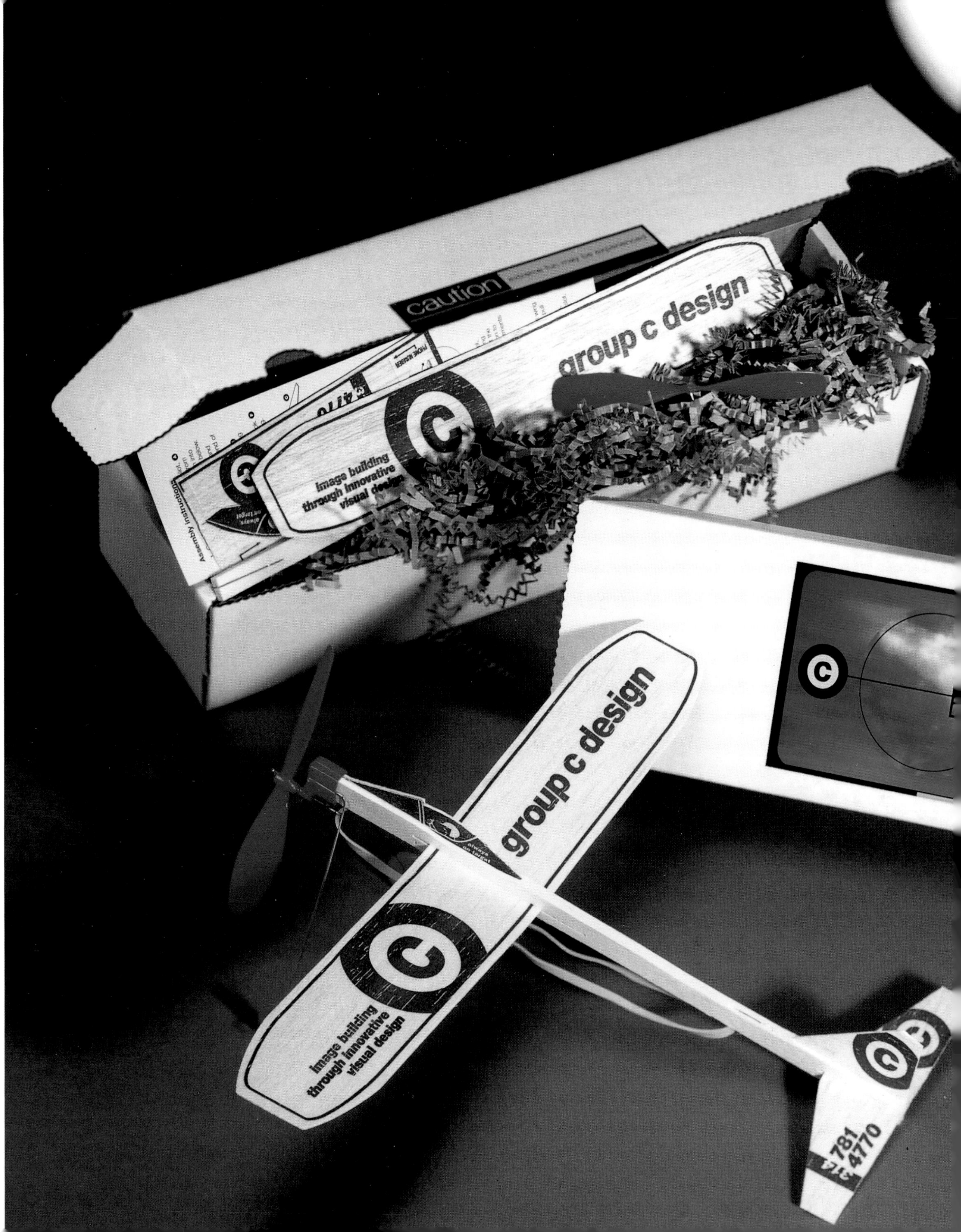
caution
group c design
image building
through innovative
visual design
781
4770

Sometimes a seemingly simple design is the most effective. The motto, "image building through innovative visual design" is offered in three-dimensional form via a propeller-powered, balsa airplane.

Package label is very strong designwise, exemplifying the firm's style and capability.

Creative Firm: Group C Design
  St. Louis, Missouri
Client: Group C Design
Business: Design firm
Creative: Benjamin Franklin

"The theme for The 1999 James Beard Foundations Annual Journalism Awards Event was 'Rising Stars of the 21st Century'. Printed in two metallic colors on white stock, the invitation had die cut stars that moved forward as the invitation was opened. A rising feel was created because of the angles that form once it was opened."

Creative Firm: John Kneapler Design
  New York, New York
Client: The James Beard Foundation
Business: Cooking foundation
Creative: John Kneapler, Michael Frizzell

42

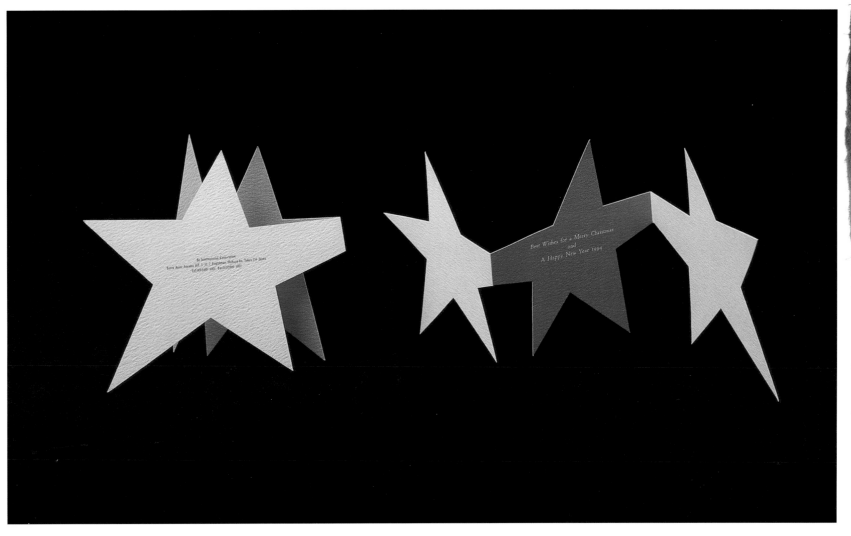

Die-cut stars fold out into this Christmas/New Year's card.

Creative Firm: Design Club
  Tokyo, Japan
Client: Be International Corporation
Business: Architectural design company
Art Director, Designer: Akihiko Tsukamoto

"Christmas 1997. The greeting headline was 'Even in 1998 we will help you make your problems less heavy. But now, enjoy your holiday.' Inside the box was found a greeting floppy, and chocolate gift consisting of a chocolate mouse and 'torrone' (almond nougat) mouse pad."

44

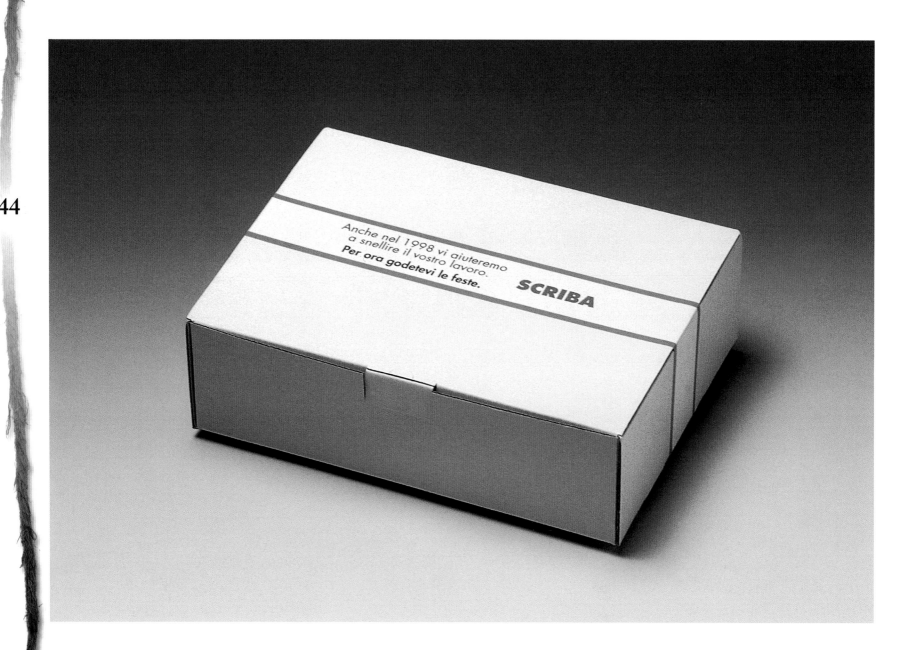

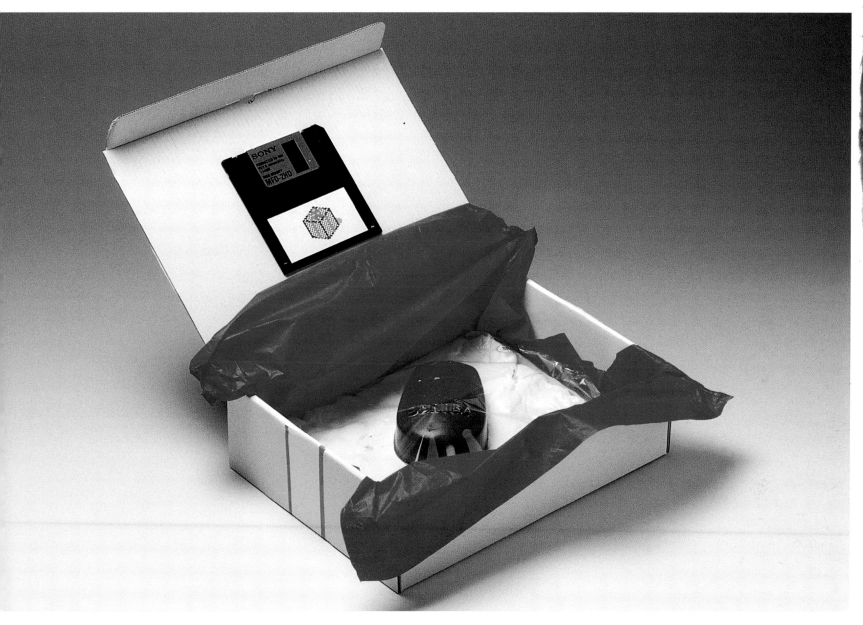

Creative Firm: Matite Giovanotte
  Forli, Italy
Client: Scriba
Business: Service for print
Copywriter: Marina Flamigni
Artist, Designer: Giovanni Pizzigati

Fortune cookies were used to promote this design firm complete with informational "fortunes" all pertaining to kor group.

Creative Firm: kor group
  Boston, Massachusetts
Client: kor group
Business: Design firm
Creative: Anne Callahan, Karen Dendy,
  MB Sawyer, Jim Gibson, Brian Acevedo

46

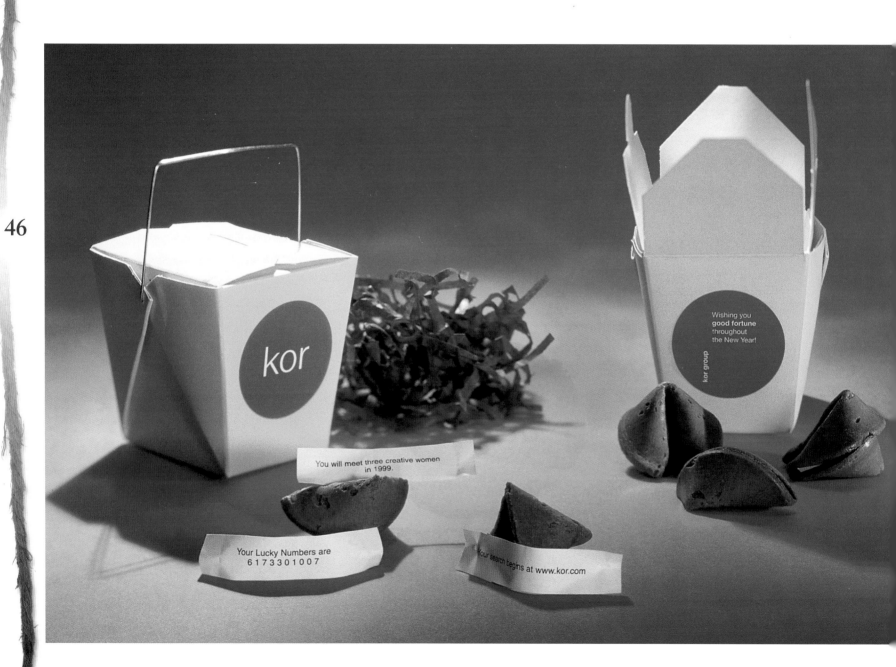

On the mug label:
FGA
FIXGO ADVERTISING (M) SDN BHD
★ FAR-OUT ★ GROOVY ★ AWESOME ★

On the left box:
SPECIALLY FOR:

WITH COMPLIMENTS FROM

FGA
FIXGO ADVERTISING (M) SDN BHD
2B, Jalan SS19/1D, Subang Jaya,
47500 Petaling Jaya, Selangor, Malaysia.
Tel: 03-7336596 Fax: 03-7331857

On the right box:
"Denim never goes out of style.
The same can be said of this
Advertising Agency.
FGA, we believe in advertising
that never goes out of style."

LET'S DRINK TO THAT!

FAR-OUT ★ GROOVY ★ AWESOME

"The FGA Denim Mug was designed as a self-promotional give away to project the timelessness of the ideas that FIXGO Advertising generates. Just like denim, which never goes out of style, the same can be said about FIXGO Advertising. They believe in advertising that never goes out of style.

"It's a philosophy you can raise a toast to!"

Creative Firm: Fixgo Advertising (M) Sdn Bhd
Subang Jaya, Malaysia Selangor
Client: Fixgo Advertising (M) Sdn Bhd
Business: Advertising
Creative: Allen Tan

"The Pin Tin was a holiday gift and self-promotion for Boelts Bros. Assoc. featuring three critter pins each designed by a partner."

Creative Firm: Boelts Bros. Assoc.
    Tucson, Arizona
Client: Boelts Bros. Assoc.
Business: Graphic design firm
Creative: Eric Boelts, Jackson Boelts,
    Kerry Stratford

Anti-Stress

Indications: For soothing relief of stress due to overworking, overthinking and overacting. Directions for use: Twist cap open. Pull out content and squeeze until too drained to feel the stress.

Warning: Do not swallow.

"To generate top-of-mind awareness for AT&T among hotel guests, and to encourage them to call via AT&T Direct Service, a premium item with appropriate packaging was designed. A minimum of calls was required to claim the gift.

"The item selected was a stress ball with an AT&T logo. As a packaging gimmick, the stress ball was placed inside a cardboard canister with the bold word 'Anti-Stress' printed on it. The packaging simulated a pill-box with a corresponding indication and warning for added humor.

"The result was that there was an increased number of AT&T Direct Service calls during the promo duration. Guests were even requesting more than one item to give away as gifts to friends."

Creative Firm: Mega Pacific
Graphic Design Inc.
Pasig City, Philippines
Client: AT&T Phils.
Business: Communication
Creative: Megpac

49

"The PRISONER T-shirt was created to mark the 25th anniversary of Risdall Linnihan Advertising. The small insignia reads '25 Years To Life' and '1972-1997' accompanied by the agency logo.

"Agency employees wore the shirts at the 25th anniversary party, to which guests were invited with mock jury-duty summonses. Guests also were given PRISONER T-shirts.

"Although the shirt was closely tied to the theme of the party, it has had an active afterlife. An agency employee who played in a straight-edge (hardcore) band routinely wore the shirt on stage, until it became excessively stained—with blood. Another sometimes wears it to mow his lawn, relishing the odd looks he gets from passersby in his upscale suburb."

Creative Firm: Risdall Linnihan Advertising
St. Paul, Minnesota
Client: Risdall Linnihan Advertising
Business: Advertising agency
Creative Director, Art Director:
Kevin O'Callaghan
Copywriters: Jenny Radack, John Risdall

51

"To promote our company's creative/marketing capabilities we created a custom mousepad and custom logo. This item was then mailed to generate qualified leads."

Creative Firm: Jack Nadel, Inc.
  Los Angeles, California
Client: Jack Nadel, Inc.
Business: Promotional advertising
Art Director, Illustrator: Scott Brown

The design of this holiday gift plays strongly on the firm's name. Printed much like a table of elements, the symbols are more fun than chemistry (and certainly better advice).

Creative Firm: Oxygen Inc.
   Chicago, Illinois
Client: Oxygen Inc.
Business: Design firm
Creative: Penina Goodman, Michelle Goldish

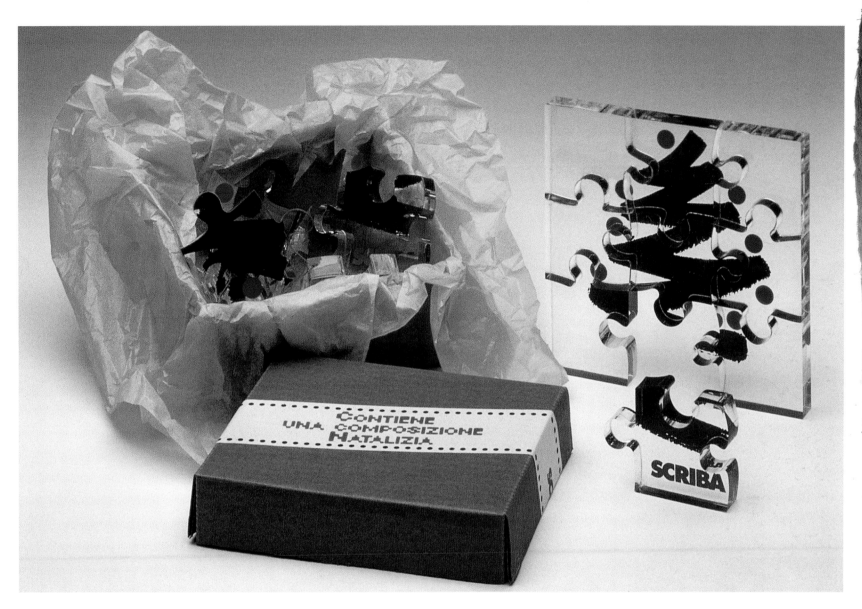

"Christmas 1995–there's a message on the gift box, 'Contiene composizione natilizia'. In Italian 'compìosizione' means both music composition and puzzle."

Creative Firm: Matite Giovanotte
  Forli, Italy
Client: Scriba
Business: Service for print
Creative: Barbara Longiardi, Giovanni Pizzigati

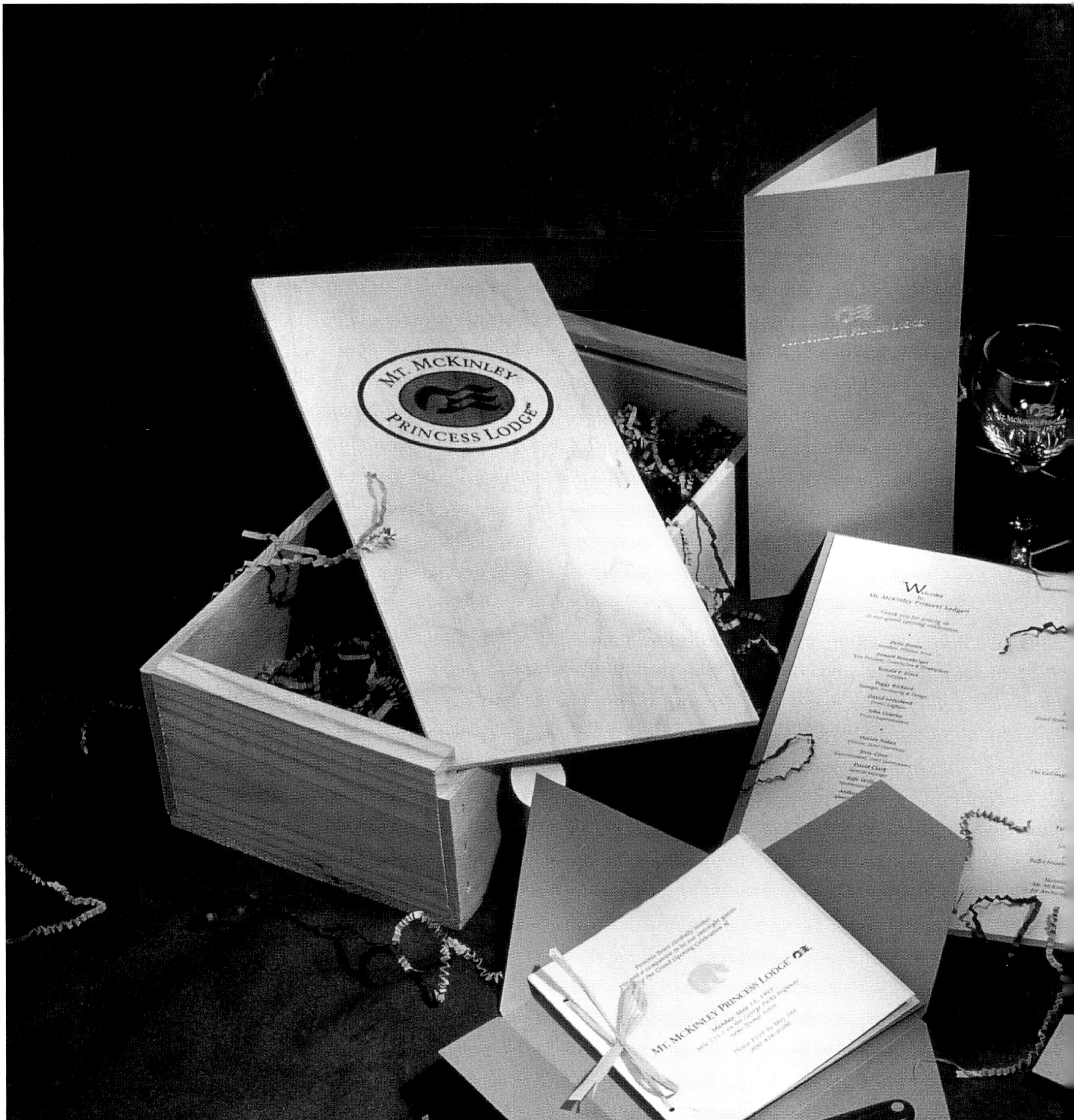
MT. MCKINLEY
PRINCESS LODGE

55

"The opening of Princess Tours' newest facility, Mt. McKinley Princess Wildness Lodge, began with a private function. Guests arrived by private train and stayed overnight. The affair included an evening event and breakfast. Belyea designed the invitations and program, and consulted on the specialty gifts."

Creative Firm: Belyea
  Seattle, Washington
Client: Princess Tours
Business: Travel company
Art Director: Patricia Belyea
Designer: Christian Salas

the Getty Opening Staff Survival Kit
Butter Toffee
Cracker Jack
STRESSED??
This coupon good for one tall latte (or equivalent) at the Coffee cart at the Getty Center Arrival Plaza
expires December 31, 1997
This coupon good for one massage at Spa Getty
Call Randy Fiel, 6215, to make an appointment
Dear
I am still su
Love,

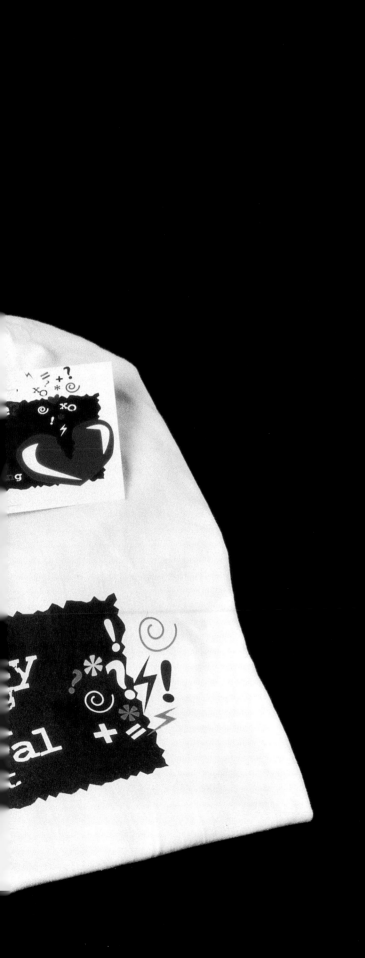

A very nice thank-you gift for the staff of the Getty Opening, everything one needs to survive a very stressful event is found in this specialty kit, including candy and aromatherapy!

Creative Firm: James Robie Design Associates
  Los Angeles, California
Client: J. Paul Getty Trust
Art Directors: James Robie, Wayne Fujita
Designer: Karen Nakatani

An interesting presentation explains the meaning of irony with respect to the tagline, "new way forward". This ties the concept of time with the gift, a watch.

Creative Firm: Watermark Associates
   Designers and Consultants Ltd.
   Hong Kong, China
Client: Hang Seng Bank
Business: Banking
Creative Director: Annie Tong
Writer: Margaret Leung

58

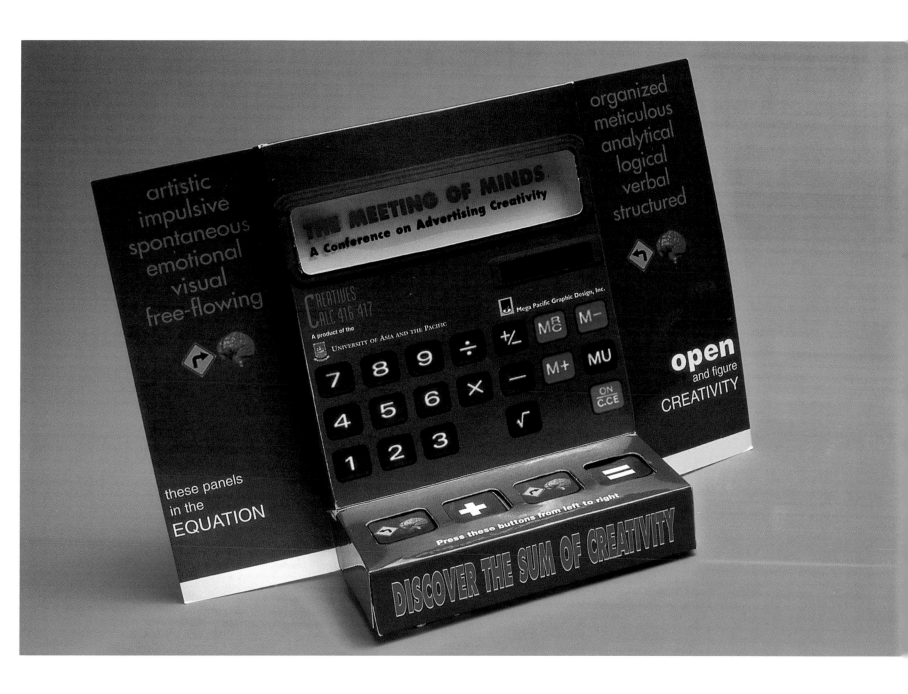

"Since this was to be given to advertising professionals who are creative themselves, the invitation had to be attention-grabbing even for these people.

"The agency designed an interactive calculator whose big idea was 'Discover the Sum of Creativity'. The recipients were instructed to press

several buttons to discover the sum of creativity. As the buttons were pressed, the screen displayed 'Left brain + Right brain ='. Then, finally, the punchline 'The Meeting of Minds A Conference on Advertising Creativity'.

"The back flaps were the conference details and sign up sheet.

"End result was a 55% attendance by advertising professionals."

Creative Firm: Mega Pacific Graphic Design Inc.
   Pasig, Philippines
Client: University of Asia & the Pacific
Business: Education
Creative: Megpac

"This 1997 mailing was sent in a small metal canister, with a string of cards inside. The small (2-1/4 inches square) box has 12 panels printed in process color."

Creative firm: BBK Studio
  Grand Rapids, Michigan
Client: The Etheridge Company
Business: Printer
Creative: Yang Kim

60

Metalmorphosis Tradeshow Invitation was
prepared with "Cu"-colored film reel case housing.
Inside, the recipient found an agent manual and
microfilm message, with "spy music" background
provided by microchip technology.

Creative Firm: Larsen Design + Interactive
   Minneapolis, Minnesota
Client: Novellus Systems, Inc.
Art Directors: Gayle Jorgens, Paul Wharton

63

"This series of bird notecards began with a photo taken by one of our designers during a walk through the neighborhood. When it came time for the studio's holiday promotional gift, we decided we wanted to create something to which the studio staff could each contribute artistically. So the photo image was digitized and given to each artist as source material. Their resulting piece became a notecard, the image being paired with a fortune that each designer found amid the piles of fortune cookies eaten during a series of lunches. The boxed set was sent at the New Year, with our wishes for good fortune, to each recipient."

Creative Firm: Kim Baer Design Associates Venice, California
Client: Kim Baer Design Associates
Business: Design firm
Creative: Kim Baer, Barbara Cooper, Maggie Van Oppen, Liz Roberts, Michael Lejeune, Helen Duval

Christmas and New Year's card (1995) uses die cuts
to create dimension with shaped edges when the
card is opened.

Creative Firm: Design Club
   Tokyo, Japan
Client: Be International Corporation
Business: Architectural Design Company
Art Director, Designer, Illustrator:
   Akihiko Tsukamoto

64

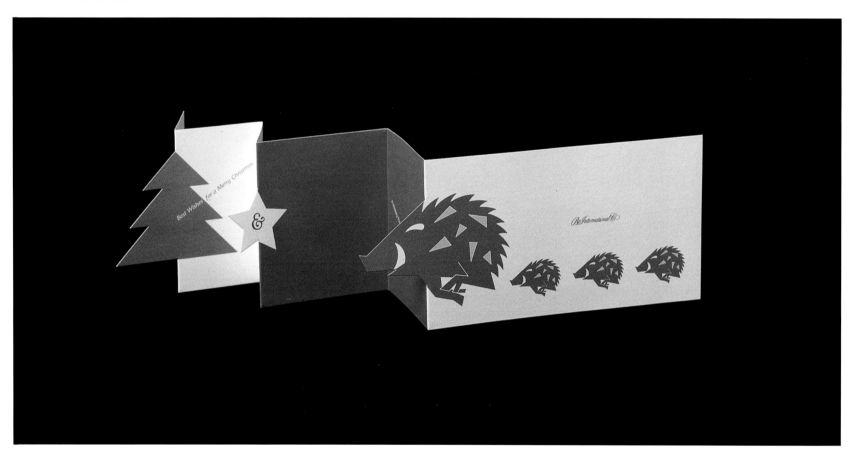

"As a way of inaugurating the new year, 1998, The Year of the Tiger, we hand-crafted our annual greeting cards to be presented to our clients. The mark of the 'Guardian Tiger' symbolized the pride of Korea. The tiger's message addresses the point of Koreans having to cooperate in a joint effort in order to unravel the country from economic distress. The appearance of the 'no frills' handmade greeting cards, which had no envelope and were sealed with masking tape, reflected the concept that we must settle down and live an humble lifestyle."

Creative Firm: DooKim Inc.
    Seoul, Korea
Client: DooKim Inc.
Business: Design company
Creative: Doo Kim

"Our studio puts together two 'gift' promotions for clients, vendors, and friends each year. The offerings are a thank-you to our business partners and a way for the studio to create as a group. Because we have a background in annual reports, where storytelling is such an effective tool for capturing a company's essence and an audience's attention, our promotions have tended to be based on a storytelling structure. 'Dearly Beloved' was born of our collective love of pets, and because so many of our friends and clients have told us interesting stories of how their pets died. The book, filled with these actual pet stories, was illustrated by one of our designers and was published in time for Halloween (All Soul's Day)."

Creative Firm: Kim Baer Design Associates
   Venice, California
Client: Kim Baer Design Associates
Business: Design firm
Art Director: Kim Baer
Designer: Barbara Cooper
Illustrator: Liz Roberts

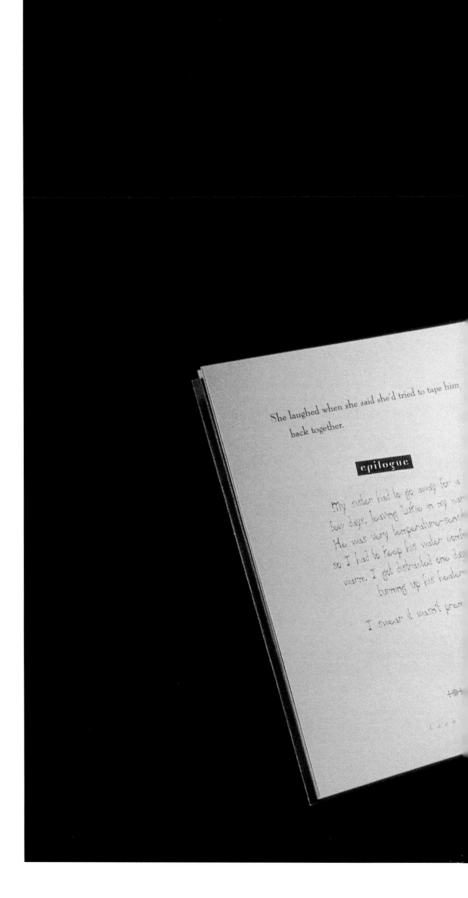

"Will Ultra Flow save you time? You can count on it." The copy is reiterated with an hourglass symbolizing both the Ultra Flow and time themes.

Creative Firm:
Gauger & Silva Associates
San Francisco, California
Client: Euromed
Creative: Isabelle Laporte, David Gauger

68

"The BBA Skinny is an announcement bound with a key chain telling of employees at the two Boelts Bros. offices in Tucson, Arizona, and Boulder, Colorado. The intended goal was one of communication to Boelts Bros. clients."

Creative Firm: Boelts Bros. Assoc.
Client: Boelts Bros. Assoc.
Business: Graphic design firm
Creative: Elicia Taylor

"To cite our recent growth as a reason for relocating to a larger office, we wanted to announce our change of address in a creative way. Utilizing a dimensional mailer also promoted our company's creative/marketing capabilities."

Creative Firm: Jack Nadel, Inc.
    Los Angeles, California
Client: Jack Nadel, Inc.
Business: Promotional advertising
Art Director, Illustrator: Scott Brown

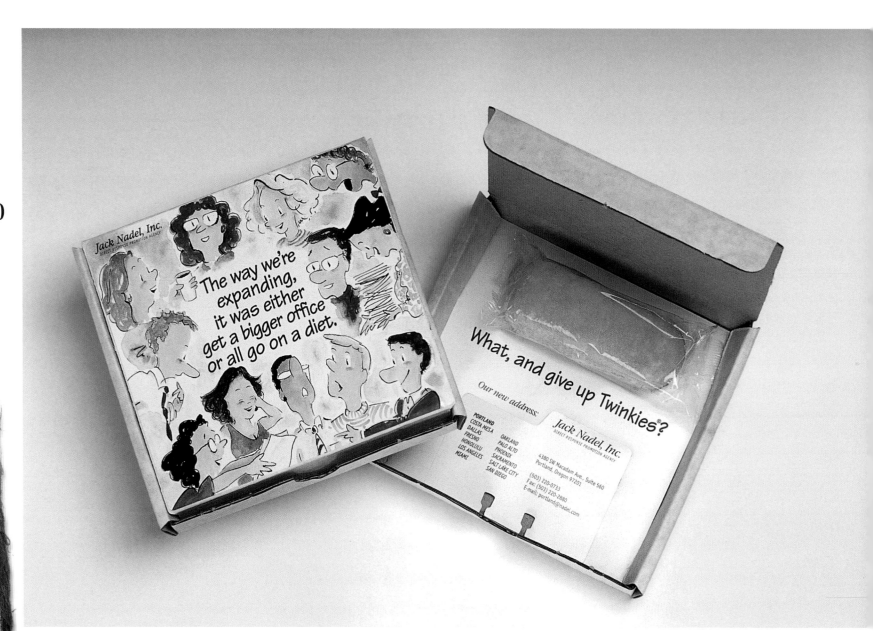

La nuova collezione
Nike Components Fall 96 ti aspetta
nei punti vendita autorizzati Nike.

Per il tuo entusiasmo,
per la tua voglia di sport,
per la tua dimensione,

in tu

COMPONENTS
Scopri la sua
vera **dimensione**
I.P.

"The press invitation for Nike Italy's new collection 1995 was a small shopping bag. The headline was 'Discover the true dimension'. When people went to the meeting, they received a bigger shopping bag."

Creative Firm: Matite Giovanotte
 Forli, Italy
Client: Nike Italy
Business: Sport shoes & equipment
Creative: Antonella Bandoli,
 Barbara Longiardi

"To usher in 1994, the Year of the Dog, we made these handmade greeting booklets. The book was composed of many famous dogs which we remember from our childhood such as those found in stories, animations, and advertisements."

WINDSOR DOG

The eternally faithful canine
companion of the Duke of
Windsor, who gave up the
throne in the name of love.

사랑을 위해 왕관을 버린 윈저공의
영원한 충견

Creative Firm: DooKim Inc.
   Seoul, Korea
Client: DooKim Inc.
Business: Design company
Creative: Doo Kim

73

MOVIE DOG

A Hollywood super dog-
Lassie, a well-known movie
star loved by millions.

영화의 주역으로 사랑을 받았던
명배우 견공 - 할리우드의 명견
래시

Calculator attached to annual report allows
stockholder to see how it all really adds up.

Creative Firm: Kompas Design d.d.
  Ljubljana, Slovenia
Client: Dolenjska Banka d.d.
Business: Banking
Art Director, Designer: Zare Kerin
Photographer: Janez Puksic

74

"This sales kit featured Love Packaging Group and its capabilities to Premier Parks, a large amusement park company (they own the Six Flags theme parks). LPG was interested in producing the collateral materials for all the amusement company's theme parks. This creative approach mimics an old-fashioned leather bound carrying case, but is actually made completely out of corrugated! It comes complete with metal trunk corners! All the collateral materials and LPG promo items were contained in this case."

Creative Firm: Love Packaging Group
   Wichita, Kansas
Client: Love Packaging Group
Business: Packaging design studio
Creative: Chris West

"The theme for The James Beard Foundation's Annual Awards Event in 1999 was 'Rising Stars of the 21st Century'. This event is the academy awards of the food industry. As the invitation is opened, the star separates itself into smaller stars."

Creative Firm: John Kneapler Design
Client: The James Beard Foundation
Business: Cooking school/foundation
Creative: John Kneapler, Michael Frizzell, Holly Buckley

76

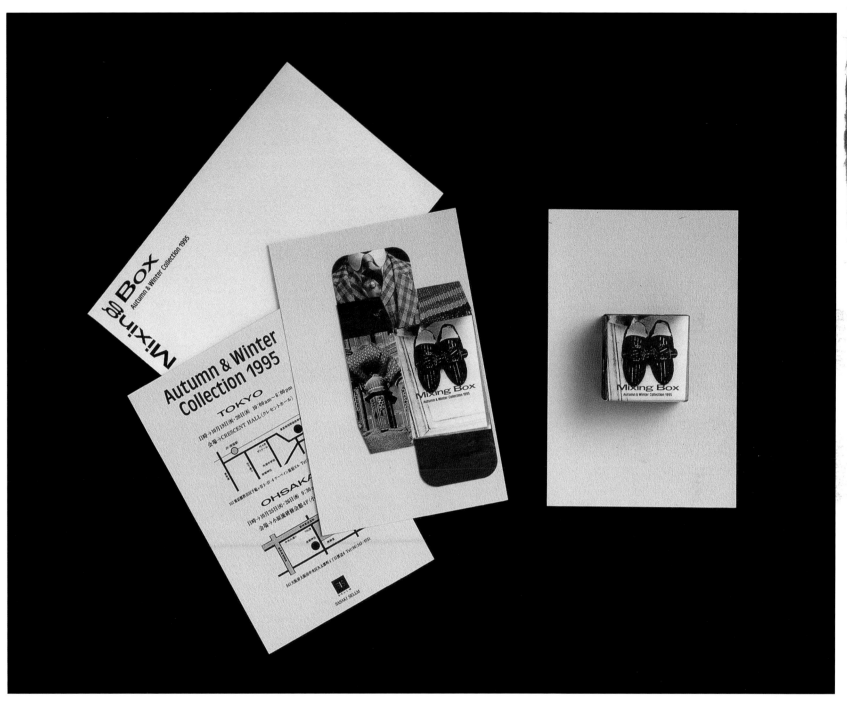

Mixing Box sent an invitation to its clientele announcing the Autumn & Winter Collection 1995. It included an actual box that could be cut out and constructed.

Creative Firm: Design Club
   Tokyo, Japan
Client: Sasaki Sellm Co., Ltd.
Business: Apparel maker
Creative Director: Setsuko Matagi
Art Director, Designer: Akihiko Tsukamoto

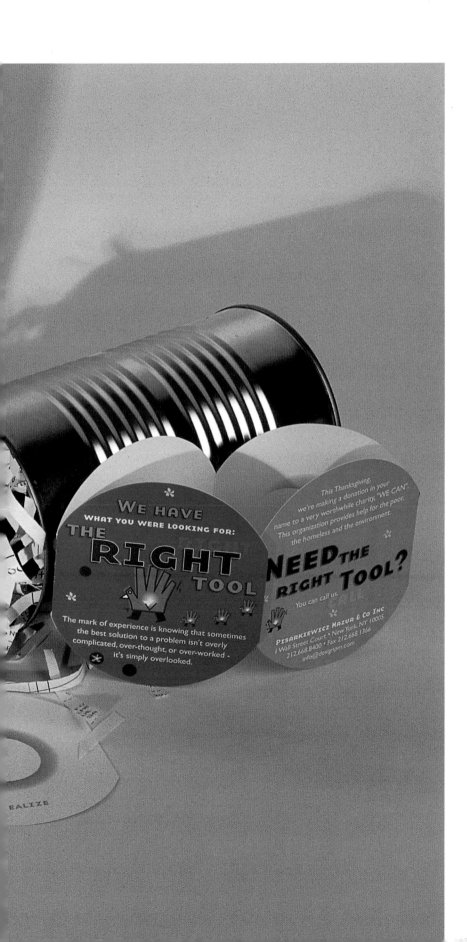

"The marketing goals and design objectives of this project were to create a memorable and unique self-promotional gift item for our present and prospective clients that communicated the value of using the right tool to solve specific marketing problems. We knew what the receiver would need to open the tin can, a can opener, finding inside a high quality, nicely designed can opener, emphasizing that some tools and solutions are simply overlooked!

"We also tied in a contribution to 'we can' in honor of the recipient's name. 'We can' is a nonprofit organization that provides food for the hungry by giving the homeless money for their collection of cans, which was appropriate both to the promotional gift and the spirit of the Thanksgiving holiday season."

Creative Firm: Pisarkiewicz Mazur & Co., Inc.
  New York, New York
Client: Pisarkiewicz Mazur & Co., Inc.
Business: Branding consultancy
Creative Director: Mary F. Pisarkiewicz
Designer: Kerstin Betzemeier

Invitations to a big blow-out celebrating 5 years of
service were printed on whoopie cushions.

Creative Firm: Sagmeister Inc.
  New York, New York
Client: Sagmeister Inc.
Business: Design company
Art Director: Stefan Sagmeister
Designers: Stefan Sagmeister, Hjalti Karlsson

80

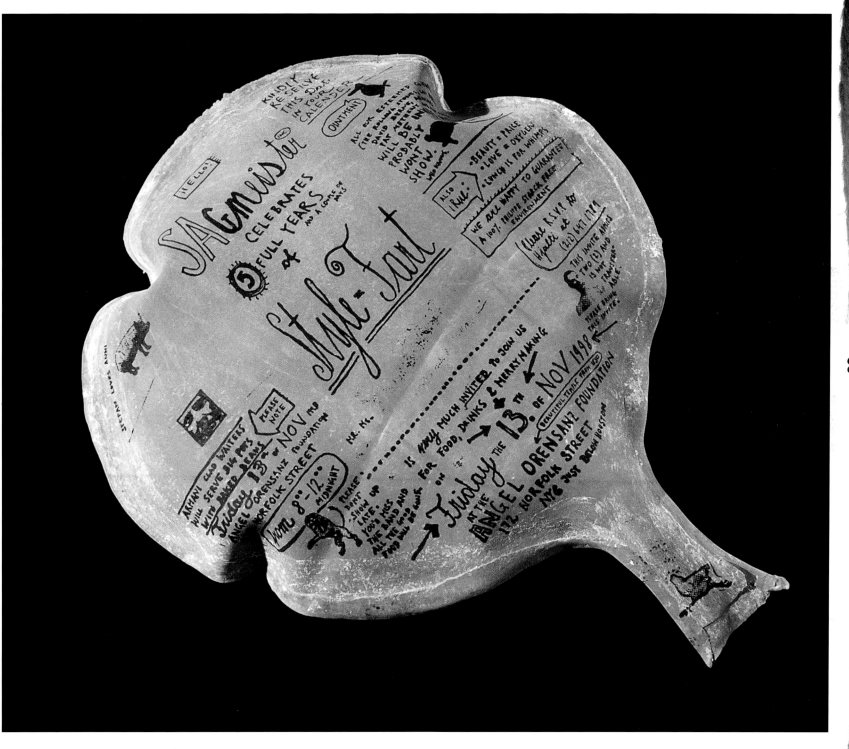

"Each year Michael Niblett Design gives a nice gift to each of its major clients for Christmas. We try to personalize the packaging of this gift so that it will also be a creative and entertaining promotion for Michael Niblett Design.

"This year a very nice bottle of Cabernet was labeled and enclosed in a custom gift box. The box simply reads Ho Ho Ho Merry Christmas. Since the bottle would never be seen in a retail setting, we designed the label to be read in 360 degrees. As you turn it in your hand, it reads 'Merry Christmas from Michael Niblett Design' or 'XXX.' Where the two messages cross, it can be read as 'Xmas.' The initial X and the labeling on the neck consist of small Ho Ho Ho's. The colors are red and a light green (sage) and black."

Creative firm: Michael Niblett Design
  Fort Worth, Texas
Client: Michael Niblett Design
Business: Design firm
Creative People: Michael Niblett

82

تأمل الحقيبة التي أمامك
CONSIDER THE CASE BEFORE YOU

"The mailer was sent to key people in companies that import goods and products on a regular basis. The objective of this piece was to inform the target audience about 'Import Express', a service from DHL that is an efficient, convenient, and cost-effective way to import goods. A DHL branded miniature briefcase (card holder) was used as a vehicle to house the information and promotional offer, and doubled as a gift. Given the target audience, the briefcase reinforced the positioning of DHL as a quality, innovative company with an answer to all their business courier needs."

Creative firm: Saatchi & Saatchi
   Dubai, United Arab Emirates
Client: DIIL
Business: Courier
Creative Director: Kurt Blanckenberg
Designer: Louise Miller

"A box of chocolates made like a floppy disk
conveyed Scriba's Christmas greetings in 1993."

Creative Firm: Matite Giovanotte
   Forli, Italy
Client: Scriba
Business: Service for print
Creative: Giovanni Pizzigati

84

85

With the popularity that the game of golf is enjoying, promotional gifts with a golf theme appeal to a vast audience.

Creative Firm:
   Gauger & Silva Associates
   San Francisco, California
Client: Euromed
Creative: Isabelle Laporte, David Gauger

"When trying to increase the sales of new PC cards, this promotion was utilized to motivate resellers and distributors of Xircom PC cards to sell them over that of the competition by awarding points toward incentive gifts (spiffs). In addition, a grand prize trip was offered to motivate 80% of the resellers who are responsible for only 20% of sales."

Creative Firm: Jack Nadel, Inc.
  Los Angeles, California
Client: Xircom
Business: Computer PC cards
Creative Director: Scott Brown
Copywriter: Sam Minster

86

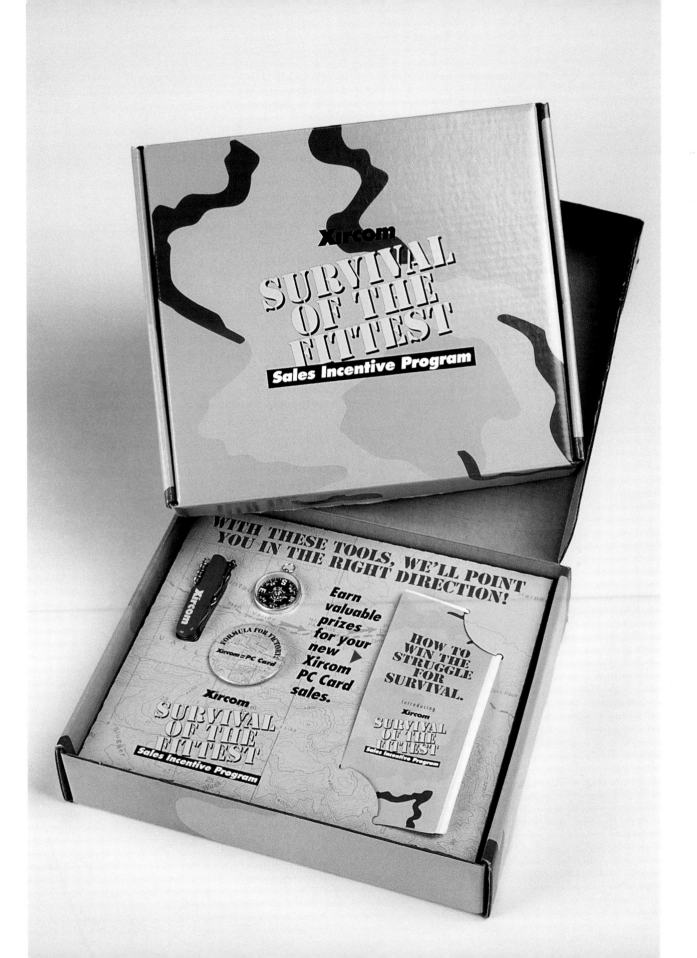

This 1999 Dealer Media Kit comes in a very nice metal case. Full of information offered in various formats, including a CD and four videos, it reiterates the high-class image for which Porsche is so well-known.

Creative Firm: Deep Design
  Atlanta, Georgia
Client: Porsche Cars North America
Designer: Mark Steingruber

"Increasing sales of Samsung digital telephones was the goal of this debit card promotion. For selling digital telephones, Samsung resellers and distributors were awarded dollar amounts which were added to their personalized debit card."

Creative Firm: Jack Nadel, Inc.
   Los Angeles, California
Client: Samsung Telecommunications America
Business: Telecommunications

Art Directors: Scott Brown, Joy Tapscott
Copywriter: Beverly Ball
Production Manager: Sam Minster

"This promotional piece promoted LPG to the restaurant market at a food and beverage tradeshow. The beverage bottles with lid labels and coaster graphics were held in the printed folding carton sleeve. Promoting LPG's ability to provide graphics for the food/beverage market and creative problem solving were shown in this fun project."

Creative Firm: Love Packaging Group
Client: Love Packaging Group
Business: Packaging design studio
Creative: Rick Gimlin

91

"Pisarkiewicz Mazur & Co. honors their clients at year end with a charitable contribution in their names and a symbolic gift. On a recent occasion, the firm chose 'Meals on Wheels' as their charity. Clients received an announcement of the contribution, along with a gift of custom-packaged honeys. The gift was accompanied by a card that described a day with an elderly shut-in whose life was brightened by a little honey in her tea and a visit from 'Meals on Wheels'."

Creative Firm: Pisarkiewicz Mazur & Co., Inc. New York, New York
Client: Pisarkiewicz Mazur & Co., Inc.
Business: Branding consultancy
Creative Director: Mary F. Pisarkiewicz
Designers: Jennifer Harenberg, Anne-Marie O'Brien
Copywriter: Bonnie Intall

A small book of photographs becomes interactive
media when tied up with a string.

Creative Firm: Kompas Design d.d.
   Ljubljana, Slovenia
Client: Rokus
Business: Publisher
Art Director, Designer: Zare Kerin
Photographer: Janez Puksic

GUITAR

TRANSDUCER

The SCHERTLER is really the only option for the guitarist sick of electric piezo-sound. If you're looking for a full-bodied bass rather than a plastic imitation, treble instead of jingle, then don't miss the chance to be a genuinely ACOUSTIC guitarist.

The transducer is attached to the body of the guitar (see the instruction booklet for details) and can be connected to stage speakers with a micro cable or directly to the mixing desk.

If you want complete control over the recording own system then the SCHERTLER ACOUSTI component linking transducer with power

The GUITAR TRANSDUCER is highly re its versatility. It is equally cello and violin as

SCHERTLER

"Schertler, a Swiss audio acoustic company, needed a brochure. The design solution included taking the concentric ellipses of the logo in a photographic direction. An actual Q-Tip was applied to the cover."

Creative Firm: Sagmeister Inc.
  New York, New York
Client: Schertler
Business: Audio acoustic manufacturer

Art Director: Stefan Sagmeister
Designers: Stefan Sagmeister, Eric Zim
Photographer: Tom Schierlitz

"To reinforce our 'Spur for Excellence' image already existing in the clients' minds, we used this direct mailer to convey the idea in a humorous manner. The three-dimensional symbol we chose was a pair of rattan, which is traditional Chinese 'equipment' for punishing kids who have made mistakes, urging them to do their best."

Creative Firm: Streamline Communication Ltd.
   Hong Kong, China
Client: Streamline Communication Ltd.
Business: Design firm
Creative Director, Art Director: Lawrence Yu
Designers: Lawrence Yu, Doris Lee
Copywriter: Grace Ip
Illustrator, Typographer: Doris Lee

94

"This program was designed for Kirk Perron of Jamba Juice, one of Hornall Anderson's current clients, for a Mediterranean cruise he hosted on a private sailboat. The Tigerlily identity was applied to a variety of special memorable gifts, which Kirk left in his guests' cabins each night to add excitement to the trip."

Creative Firm: Hornall Anderson Design Works
 Seattle, Washington
Client: Tigerlily
Business: Mediterranean cruise
Art Directors: Jack Anderson, Lisa Cerveny
Designers: Jack Anderson, Lisa Cerveny,
 Sonja Max, Mary Hermes

"This greeting card for 1992, the Year of the Monkey, was presented in the manner of a corporate identity manual with the monkey being the primary symbol. By his expressions, you see the monkey in various applications. It reflects our professionalism while adding a touch of humor to the holidays."

Creative Firm: DooKim Inc.
  Seoul, Korea
Client: DooKim Inc.
Business: Design company
Creative: Doo Kim

Corporate Symbol

Grid System

Signature & Color Scheme

MONKEY'92

Monkey Red

Monkey Gray

Incorrected Symbol

MONKEY'92

MONKEY'92

MONKEY'92

"For commercial radio station Radio 2UE, this sales promotion kit came in a metal box with radio dial."

Creative Firm: Emery Vincent Design
  Southbank, Australia
Client: Radio 2UE
Creative: Emery Vincent Design team

"This unique rubberband-activated polygon pop-up calendar instantly springs to life when removed from the mailing envelope. The elegant treatment of the graphics allowed this piece to transcend initial use as a calendar. It became an object of art to those who received it. And though the calendar year was over, people kept it on their desks—making it a continuous reminder of the sender."

Creative Firm: Tom Fowler, Inc.
   Stamford, Connecticut
Client: Tom Fowler, Inc.
Business: Graphic designers
Creative: Thomas G. Fowler

100

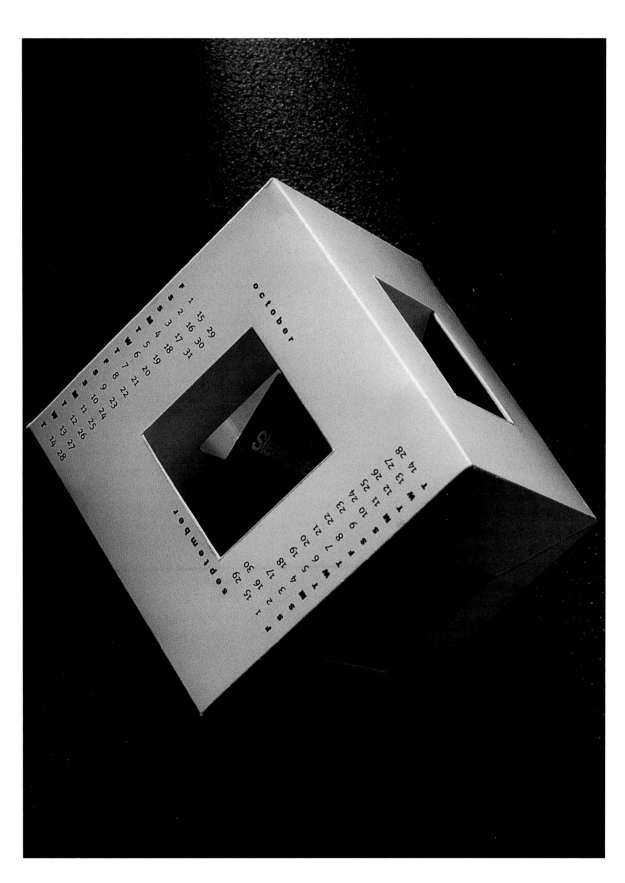

"Three-dimensional calendar was chosen to promote Steecase."

Creative Firm: Emery Vincent Design
  Southbank, Australia
Client: Steelcase Design
Business: Office furniture manufacturer
Creative: Emery Vincent Design team

Playing on the theme of internationality, flags of
many lands with a display stand are included in this
promotional kit. Each flag has a card with specific
copy for the targeted country.

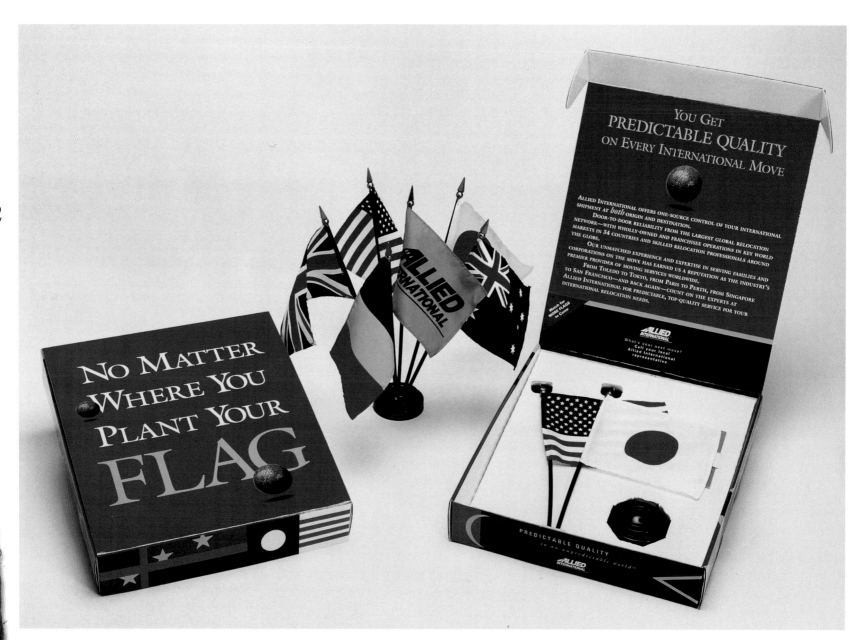

103

Creative Firm: Meindl & Associates
  Oak Brook, Illinois
Client: Allied Van Lines (International)
Business: Movers
Creative Service: Beth Keller Stein
Editorial Service: Dave Niemi
Copywriter: Martin Kantor

Using actual photographs shot for Easton Sports, Inc., original baseball cards were created. This provided the unifying idea behind the promotional package which included a ball cap, peanuts, t-shirt, and pennant.

Creative Firm: Visual Asylum
San Diego, California
Client: Jonothan Woodward
Photography
Business: Photography
Art Directors: MaeLin Levine,
Amy Jo Levine
Designers: Joel Sotelo, Charles Glaubitz,
Paul Drohan

104

"The 'Registration Rewards Chip-in & Win' promotion was announced with a portable golf course and Cisco Systems golf ball—a reminder of chipping it in. The marketing goal was to sell and register online the end users of CISCO SMARTnet service contracts to earn points for valuable prizes."

Creative Firm: Jack Nadel, Inc.
  Los Angeles, California
Client: Cisco Systems
Business: Internet hardware developers
Art Directors: Scott Brown, Jack Mongo
Copywriter: Robert Buckingham
Illustrator: Scott Brown
Website Designer: JETU

"Designer" coffee is offered by this firm.
Corrugated bags, and stamped tags tied on with
six-skein embroidery floss give this promotion a
hands-on feel. Label copy is very humorous and
complements the entire package.

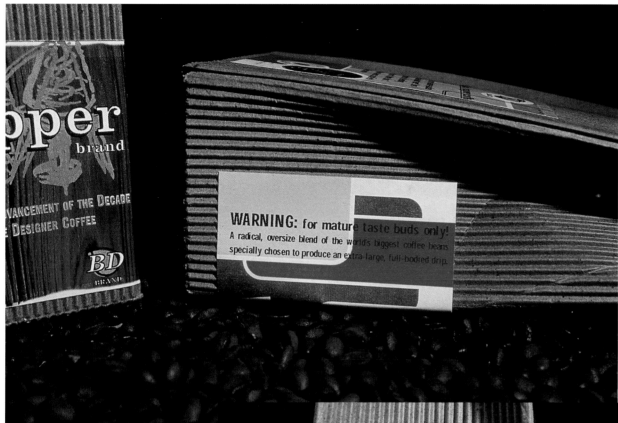

WARNING: for mature taste buds only!
A radical, oversize blend of the world's biggest coffee beans specially chosen to produce an extra-large, full-bodied drip.

Creative Firm: Aartvark
   Communications
   Vanier, Canada
Client: Aartvark Communications
Business: Design firm
Art Directors: Jean-Luc Denat
Designers and Electronic
Artwork: Jean-Luc Denat,
   Etienne Bessette

"The Hornall Anderson Design Works online direct mail 'bottle' promo was designed to introduce potential clients and partners to HADW's work, capabilities, team, and design/development philosophy by guiding them to the firm's new website.

"A bottle was used to reflect the 'message in a bottle' idea for sending the tag bearing just the firm's web site URL address."

Creative Firm: Hornall Anderson Design Works
  Seattle, Washington
Client: Hornall Anderson Design Works
Business: Graphic design firm
Art Director: Jack Anderson
Designers: Jack Anderson, Chris Sallquist,
  John Anicker, Mary Hesler, Shawn Sutherland

"Town & Country Linen was changing both its name and the location of its New York showroom. PM&Co. had created the company's entire new identity campaign which culminated in a special communication to customers and prospects. The announcement took the form of a gift package containing a rock paperweight carved with the new element of the client's name—'Living' and their familiar initials 'T&C'. An enclosed card explained that Town & Country was leaving 'no stone unturned' in informing their customers of their new name and their address (which is just a 'stone's throw' from their old showroom.)"

Creative Firm: Pisarkiewicz Mazur & Co., Inc.
  New York, New York
Client: Town & Country Living
Business: Manufacturer of home
  fashion accessories
Creative Director: Mary F. Pisarkiewicz
Designer: Jennifer Harenberg
Copywriter: Bonnie Intall

"This self-promotional brochure is a series of case studies of Boelts Bros.' clients and projects to send to both existing and potential clients."

110

111

Creative Firm:
  Boelts Bros. Assoc.
  Tucson, Arizona
Client: Boelts Bros. Assoc.
Business: Graphic design firm
Creative: Jackson Boelts,
  Eric Boelts, Kerry Stratford

"The FGA Hand-Out Stationary Holder was designed to provide a promotional giveaway that both reminds people about FIXGO Advertising while providing functionality.

"Offering a hands-on approach, it gives clients a daily reminder that FIXGO Advertising is always on-hand to provide strategic solutions.

"This hands-on solution to self promotion has proven itself to be a true hands down winner for FIXGO Advertising."

Creative Firm: Fixgo Advertising (M) Sdn Bhd
   Subang Jaya, Malaysia
Client: Fixgo Advertising (M) Sdn Bhd
Business: Advertising
Creative: Allen Tan

"The Tootsie Roll Millennium Bank promotion was developed as a playful campaign by Tootsie Roll Industries, Inc. to promote their banks filled with delicious Tootsie Roll candies. As the new millennium approaches, more and more people have become concerned about Y2K compliance. The twist is Tootsie Roll Millennium Banks are Y2K compliant. It is a special treat because of its dual usage. After enjoying the bite size Tootsie Rolls, one can also enjoy the peace of mind that comes with knowing the future of the economy does not effect any money in a Tootsie Roll Millennium Bank."

Creative Firm: Design Resource Center
Naperville, Illinois
Client: Tootsie Roll Industries, Inc.
Business: Candy company
Creative: John Norman

A great keepsake commemorating the inaugural season of the Arizona
Diamondbacks included season tickets and VIP pass. Personalized brass plaque
attached to inside of box lid is a nice touch.

Creative Firm: SRO Communications
    Phoenix, Arizona
Client: Arizona Diamondbacks
Business: Professional baseball team
Creative Director: Deb Graham
Production: Page One Production,
    Arnold Anderson, Charles Baugh
Production Manager: Sharon Bruton

114

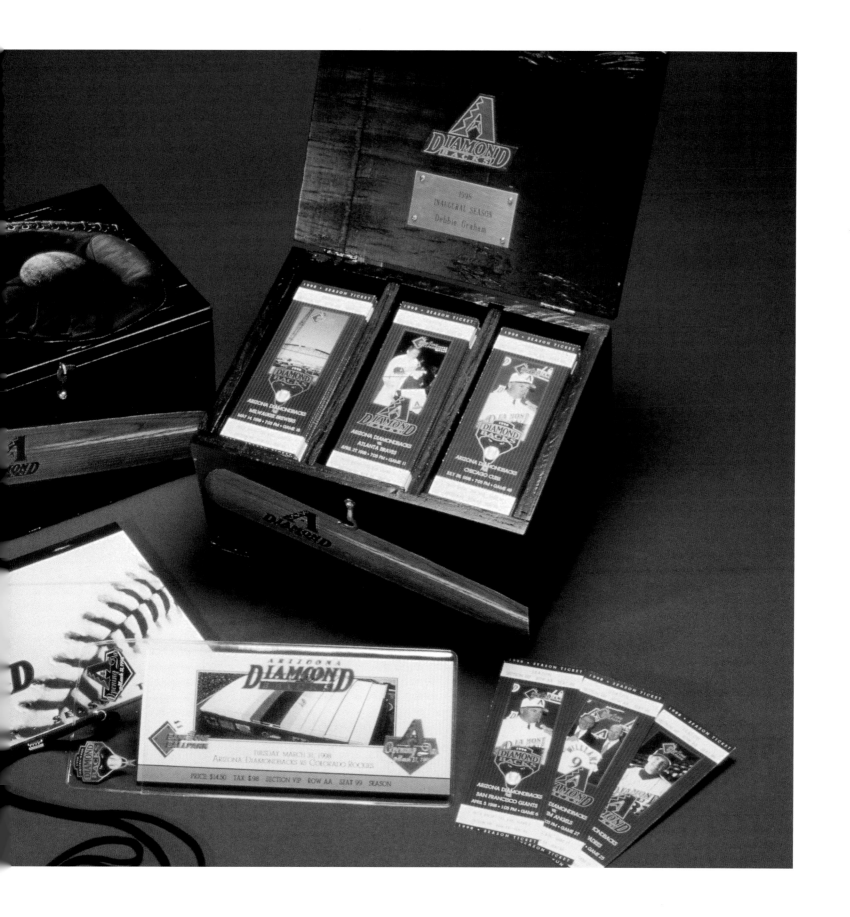

"Your piece of the pie" campaign arrived in a pizza box. Employee stock ownership and savings plan information was found inside with a booklet and video tape.

Creative Firm:
   Tom Dolle Design
   New York, New York
Client: Marjorie Gross + Co. for UICI
Creative Director:
   Marjorie Gross
Designers: Tom Dolle, Jana Paterson, Chris Riely

116

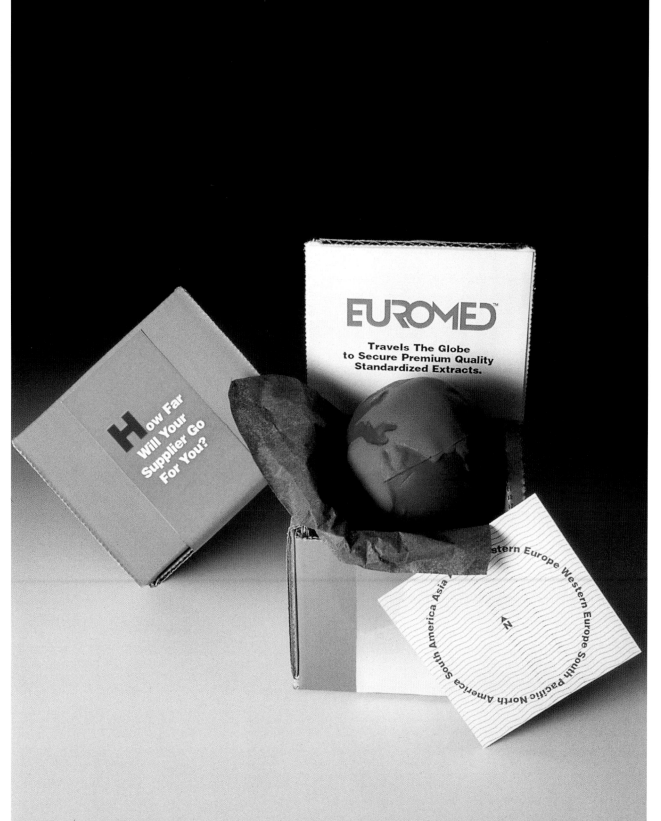

EUROMED

Travels The Globe
to Secure Premium Quality
Standardized Extracts.

How Far
Will Your
Supplier Go
For You?

117

To stress that Euromed would
go to the ends of the earth for
its clientele, a stress ball in the
shape and colors of a globe was
devised as the central item in
this promotional mailing.

Creative Firm:
  Gauger & Silva Associates
  San Francisco, California
Client: Euromed
Creative: Isabelle Laporte,
  David Gauger

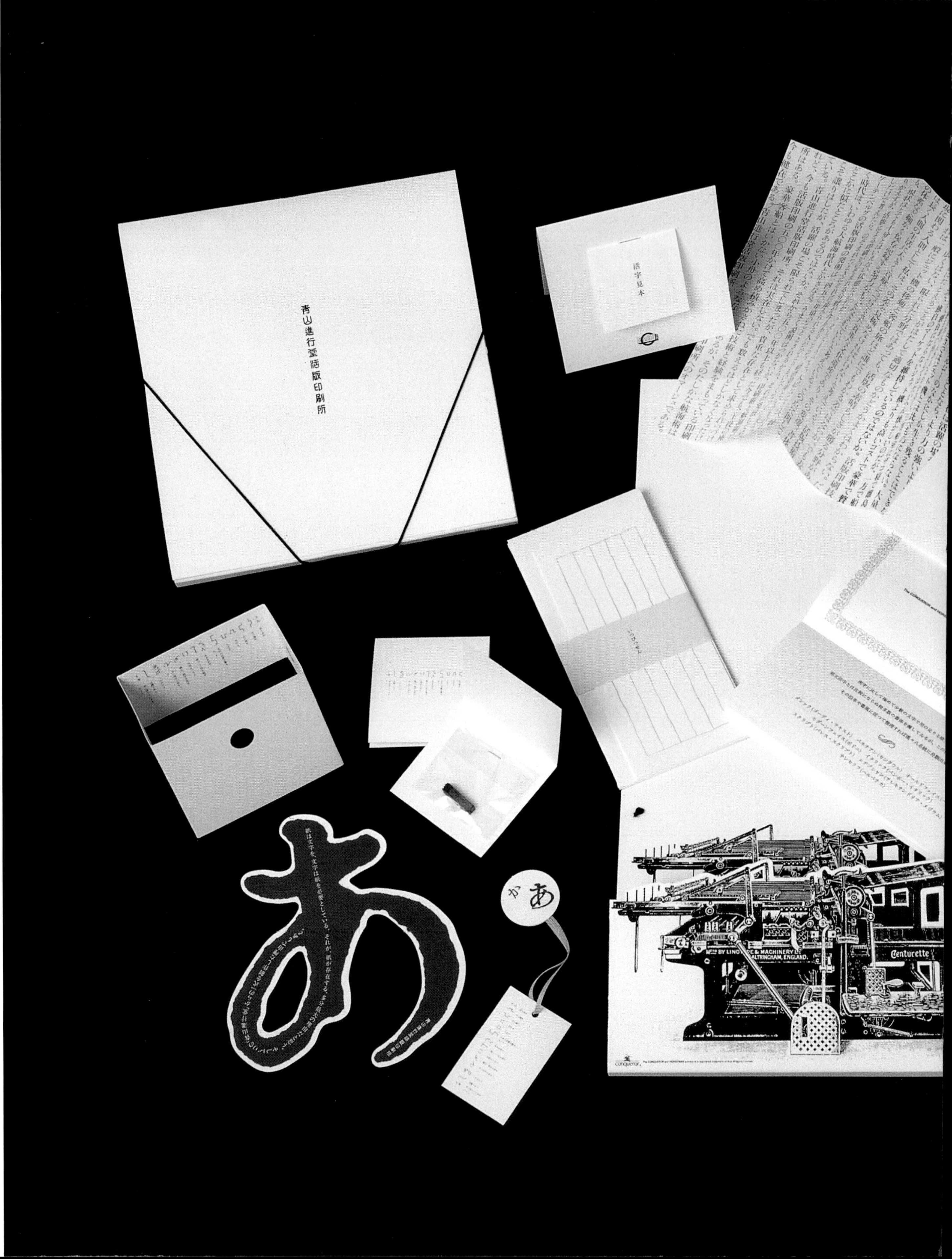
青山進行堂活版印刷所
活字見本
Centurette

119

To promote their "Conqueror" paper, this sample pack was put together for vendors. It's full of ideas for printing and using the paper in a three-dimensional format.

Creative Firm: Design Club
  Tokyo, Japan
Client: Arjo Wiggins Fine Paper Ltd.
Business: Paper manufacturer
Art Director, Designer: Akihiko Tsukamoto
Copywriter: Haruki Nagumo
Special Thanks: The Kazui Press Ltd.,
  TRI Company Limited

"Merck's public relations firm, Innerscience, approached us to create a unique and innovative way of announcing their new product to the media. The new product is Maxalt—a migraine headache pill that dissolves on your tongue as it rushes to relieve migraine headache pain. The spinning folds unravel to show the pills inside as a quick way of getting right to the source of the pain. The package was used as a press kit to educate the media about this new product."

Creative Firm: John Kneapler Design
   New York, New York
Client: Innerscience PR/Merck
Business: Public relations firm/pharmaceuticals
Creative: John Kneapler, Holly Buckley

120

"With a couple of simple folds, the viewer can turn this card into a working sundial. This card was just printed in a limited run of 2000 for our studio as a self promotion. (The sundial gives the correct time anywhere in the U.S.!)"

Creative Firm: Sagmeister Inc.
New York, New York
Client: Sagmeister Inc.
Business: Design company
Art Director: Stefan Sagmeister
Designers: Stefan Sagmeister, Veronica Oh

"By the time the celebrity recipients of this unique fundraising invitation for the International Glass Museum opened the shiny silver canister to discover a silver-printed, tissue-wrapped cobalt and silver glass objet d'art, how could they ignore the coiled-paper invitation to attend a gala reception and make a major gift to this world center for glass art?"

Creative Firm: The Traver Company
   Seattle, Washington
Client: International Glass Museum
Business: Glass museum
Creative: Anne Traver, Christopher Downs

123

"Everyone was ready with a 'high-five' to greet 1995. To keep all their clients' hands and fingers happy and healthy, PM&Co. sent a special New Year's gift of soothing, natural herbal soaks and creams formulated especially for the hands. Accompanying the gift was a custom-designed booklet reminding the recipients of the value of work done by hand (even if those hands are moving a mouse or keying in a computer command). And, in the PM&Co. tradition, a contribution is made in the client's name to a charity. The Multiple Sclerosis Society was 1995's beneficiary."

Creative Firm: Pisarkiewicz Mazur & Co., Inc.
   New York, New York
Client: Pisarkiewicz Mazur & Co., Inc.
Business: Branding consultancy
Creative Director: Mary F. Pisarkiewicz
Designer: Joe D'Zialo

124

"This was an invitation to a Tucson, Arizona, office promotion party announcing a new branch office in Boulder, Colorado."

Creative Firm: Boelts Bros. Assoc.
  Tucson, Arizona
Client: Boelts Bros. Assoc.
Business: Graphic design firm
Creative: Eric Boelts, Jackson Boelts,
  Kerry Stratford

Die-cut cover is the first level of dimension in the
booklet. Beyond that, vellum sheets are used,
creating levels of depth in a relatively flat space.

126

Creative Firm: Inox Design
   Milano, Italy
Client: Zanders (Papermill)
Designers: Mauro Pastore, Claudio Gavazzi

"The Deafness Foundation was selected by Pisarkiewicz Mazur & Co. by which PM&Co. could honor their clients with a charitable contribution. Clients received an announcement of this Thanksgiving contribution along with a custom-packaged fun gift—a classic wild turkey caller. The old-fashioned hunting device reminded the clients of the rewards of clear communication."

Creative Firm: Pisarkiewicz Mazur & Co.
  New York, New York
Client: Pisarkiewicz Mazur & Co.
Business: Branding consultancy
Creative Director: Mary F. Pisarkiewicz
Designer: Andy Geroski

"The AOPA Golf Promo was an advertising
promotion for AOPA Pilot Magazine. AOPA is
the Aircraft Owners and Pilots Association, a
nationwide organization."

Creative Firm: Boelts Bros. Assoc.
 Tucson, Arizona
Client: AOPA Pilot Magazine
Business: Aircraft owners & pilots association
Creative: Eric Boelts, Jackson Boelts,
 Kerry Stratford

"It's the holidays. Potato season, if you work at After Hours Creative. Each holiday season, the agency creates a hands-on activity that not only serves as a 'thank you' gift to its clients, but doubles as a family activity. This past year, the firm mailed real potatoes, paints, a carving knife, large blank sheets of paper, and a jumbo poster of a potato—the instruction guide to making hand-stamped holiday wrapping paper."

Creative Firm:
   After Hours Creative
   Phoenix, Arizona
Client: After Hours Creative
Business: Design firm
Creative: After Hours Creative

130

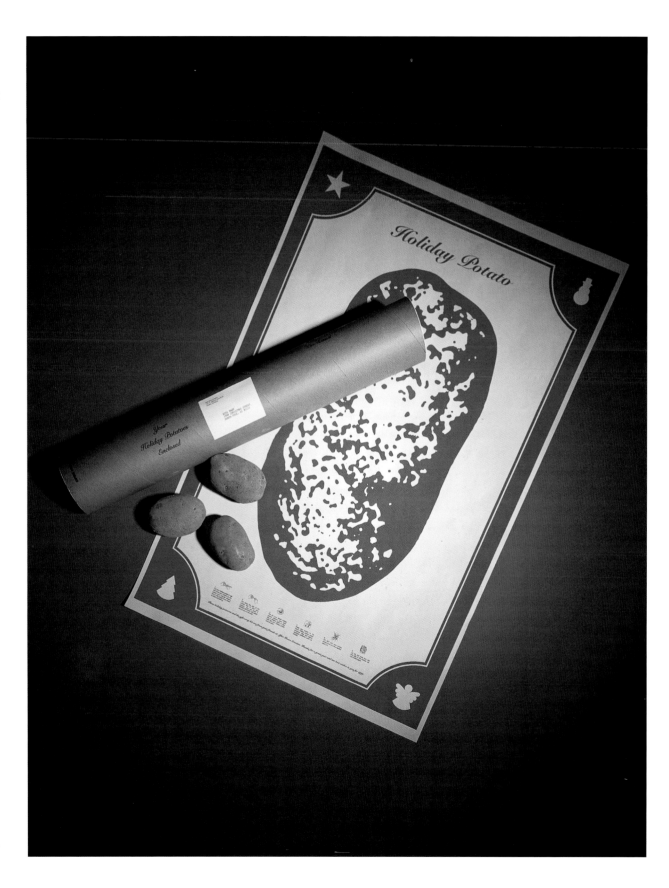

For the Innovative Thinking Conference, this original clipboard was developed. Made of wood, it includes a "built-in" handle for easy transport. The bottom edge is curved so it might be supported against the user's body in a comfortable manner.

Creative Firm:
SHR Perceptual Management
Scottsdale, Arizona
Client: Innovative Thinking Conference
Designer:
Christopher Nagle

132

"This sales kit featured Interex and its new 'Travel Surge' surge adaptor to the wholesale market at the industrial trade show. Original travel 'stickers' were designed and placed on the corrugated box that looked like a well-traveled suitcase. Interex was interested in grabbing attention to the new product in their family of computer accessories. The fun appeal of the travel case led to great success."

Creative Firm: Love Packaging Group
   Wichita, Kansas
Client: Interex
Business: Computer accessories manufacturer
Creative: Dustin Commer

The Kona Coast Promotion, "Escape to the Elements", included natural colors, seashells and sea grass used in the packaging.

134

135

Creative Firm: Gardner Design
  Wichita, Kansas
Client: Doskocil
Art Directors, Designers: Bill Gardner,
  Brian Miller

"The AOPA Hot Sauce Promo was an announcement for an AOPA Pilot Magazine party with a Cajun theme."

Creative Firm: Boelts Bros. Assoc.
    Tucson, Arizona
Client: AOPA Pilot Magazine
Business: Aircraft owners & pilots association
Creative: Eric Boelts, Jackson Boelts,
    Kerry Stratford

136

"PM&Co. honors their clients at year end with a charitable contribution in their names and symbolic gift. A foundation for Native American children was one recent recipient. Clients received an announcement of the contribution, along with a custom-designed gift package—a traditional canning jar filled with corn on the cob for popping. The gift was accompanied by a card describing the foundation and reminding the clients that corn was one of the first gifts of the Native Americans to the European settlers."

Creative Firm: Pisarkiewicz Mazur & Co., Inc.
  New York, New York
Client: Pisarkiewicz Mazur & Co., Inc.
Business: Branding consultancy
Creative Director: Mary F. Pisarkiewicz
Designers: Andy Geroski, Mary Maggio, Jennifer King
Copywriter: Peter Vogt

"This sales kit featured Love Packaging Group and its creative possibilities at the automotive tradeshow. The metal toolbox really is made completely from corrugated! The toolbox holds various collateral items including this unique 'oil can' which contains a custom-silkscreened, red auto rag with the LPG logo, and a rolled-up capabilities brochure. Overall great reviews and huge sales response made this unique and witty solution a real winner."

Creative Firm: Love Packaging Group
   Wichita, Kansas
Client: Love Packaging Group
Business: Packaging design studio
Creative: Dustin Commer

138

139

This promotional clock not only tells time by the hour; it serves as a calendar as well with the use of interchangeable clock faces.

Creative Firm: Paprika Communications
  Montréal, Canada
Client: Paprika/Litho Acme
Business: Graphic design/Printer
Art Director: Louis Gagnon
Designer: Francis Turgeon
Prepress, Printing: Litho Acme

"This kit is a high-impact piece to promote Cisco's latest line of high-performance, multilayer switches that support intelligent networking, multimedia, and converging data, voice, and video. Components assault all the senses, including unexplained phenomenon, B&W photos, circular slide rule code breaker, 24-page brochure, passport, and 12-minute audio featuring an original soundtrack, sound effects, and three actors' voices. The C-Force of intelligent Cats, the familiar abbreviation for the Catalyst Series of Switches, is loosely based on the X-Files characters, with traces of Mission Impossible and James Bond.

"The C-Force Kit was designed with three audiences in mind: the Cisco Sales Force, the high-tech press, and Cisco customers. The product roll-out also featured Cisco's first live Webcast, which tied into the C-Force look. Our previous high-impact piece for the Catalyst series helped a similar product line go from $0 in sales to $1 billion in the first 12 months!"

Creative Firm: Wong•Wong•Boyack, Inc.
   San Francisco, California
Client: Cisco Systems, Inc.
Business: Computer networking
Creative: Ben Wong, Penelope Wong,
   Homan Lee, Pagely Tucker,
   Yolanda Petriz Morris,
   Phuong-Mai Bui-Quang

"KBDA created this die-cut pyramid as a unique way to introduce the new identity that the studio had designed for Embry Press, a small but very high-quality print house in Los Angeles. The pyramid includes informational stories on the meaning of the letter 'E' throughout history, relating the letterform to the design of the new identity package that was also included in the mailing. The promotion continues to be used for new and potential customer contact."

Creative Firm: Kim Baer Design Associates
    Venice, California
Client: Embry Press
Business: Printing
Art Director: Kim Baer
Designer: Barbara Cooper

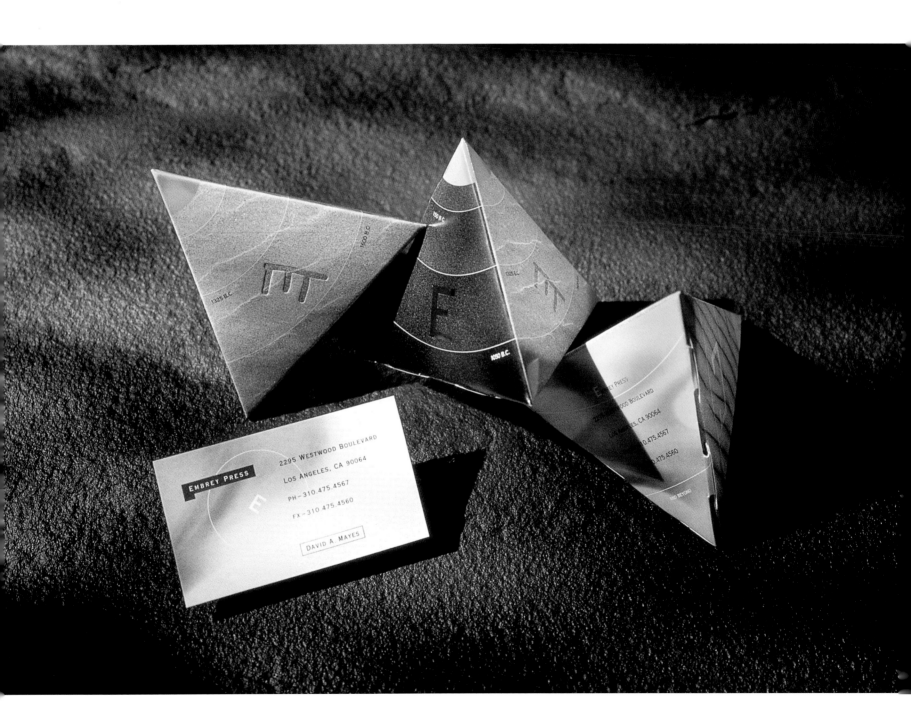

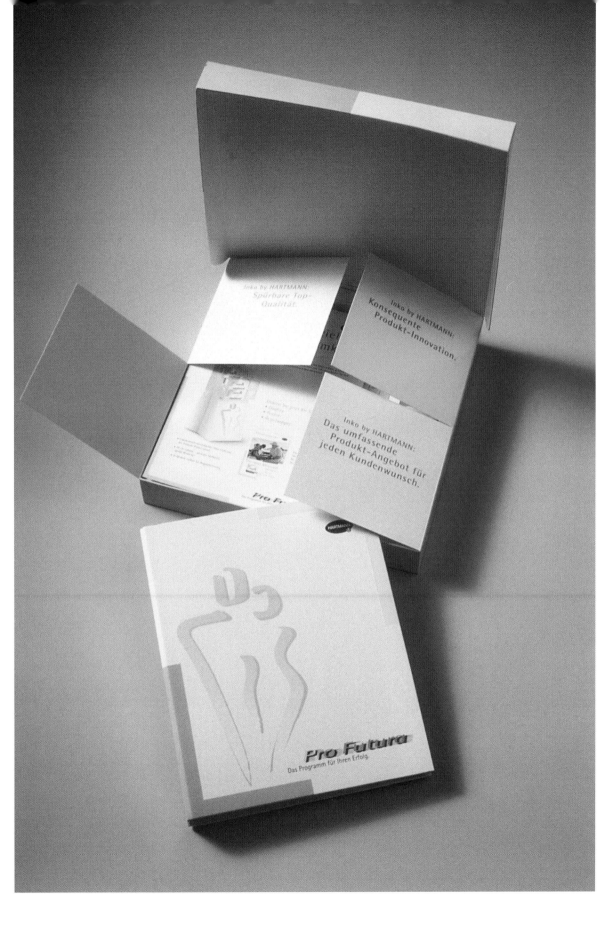

143

"Paul Hartmann AG, Heidenheim, Germany, is one of the leading European producers of medical and hygiene products. The idea and the concept for the innovative dialogue-program, 'Pro Futura', for pharmacies and specialized retailers, were developed by Fritsch Heine Rapp Collins, Hamburg. The theme of the information and education campaign is incontinence. The aim is to sensitize the target group for incontinence to support their consultancy-service and to position the Paul Hartmann AG as the leading specialist in the field."

Creative Firm: Fritsch Heine Rapp Collins
  Hamburg, Germany
Client: Paul Hartmann AG
Business: Producer of medical and
  hygiene products
Creative: Fritsch Heine Rapp Collins

"A promotional brochure for Canson-Talens, Inc., a leading producer of fine quality art and printing papers, was designed for their Canson Satin—a superior translucent sheet that can be used in an endless variety of ways, adding a dimension of excitement that no other ordinary or translucent sheet can approach.

"The brochure is made with innovative typography and imagery which demonstrate the beauty of the stock. Within the brochure is a tipped in sheet of Canson Satin that has been printed, scored, and die cut. By following the attached instruction, the viewer can assemble their own Canson Satin box, thereby demonstrating the unique strength and compelling interest of the stock itself."

144

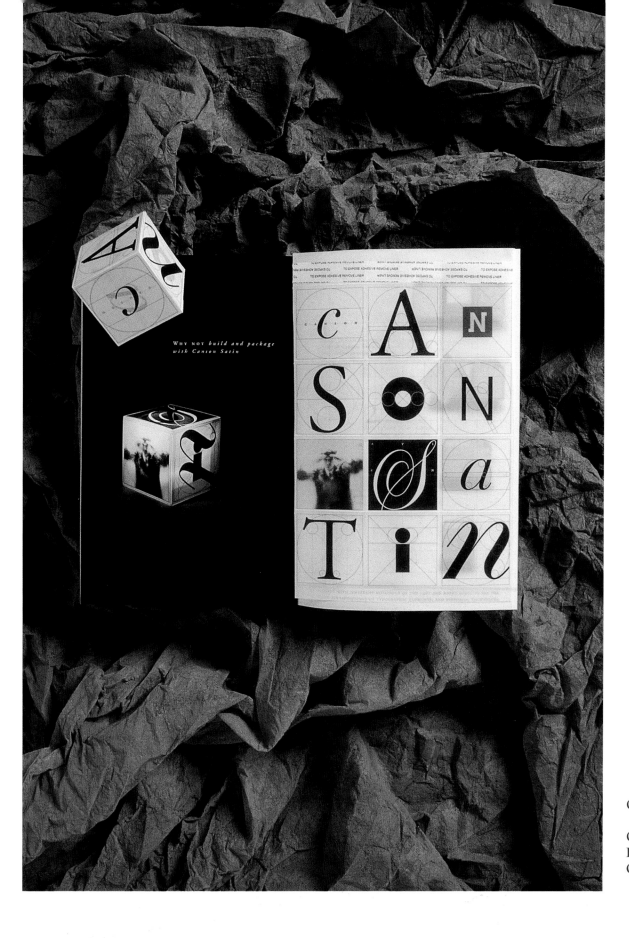

Creative Firm: Tom Fowler, Inc.
  Stamford, Connecticut
Client: Canson-Talens, Inc.
Business: Paper manufacturer
Creative: Thomas G. Fowler,
  Karl Maruyama, Brien O'Reilly

"To premier Unitel's 'Gold' vehicle, the client requested a credential pass be mailed out with the invitation for reasons of security."

Creative Firm: IE Design
  Studio City, California
Client: Unitel Mobile
Business: Video production vehicle manufacturer
Designer: Marcie Carson

146

147

"Excel is the meat processing division of the Cargill Corporation, and every year they hold a sales and staff motivational program/event. This year the theme for the meeting was 'Sometimes Opportunity Knocks…Sometimes You Have to Knock For It…' The piece we were to design was a giveaway/reminder that reinforced the conference theme. Immediately we knew that a door knocker was the right image, but how to achieve the unexpected was the real challenge. We explored several styles of rendering and combinations of materials—and even contemplated using actual brass door knockers before arriving at our solution. It came in right on budget and easily translated into t-shirts for further promotions. Response was overwhelming. The Excel employees had never received anything as substantial at any of the past meetings, and the door knocker awards/giveaways are visible all throughout their offices on tables and desktops—always providing an opening for sales people to explain the aggressive/progressive attitude of Excel."

Creative Firm: Gardner Design
　　Wichita, Kansas
Client: Excel
Business: Meat processing, sales, distribution
Art Directors, Designers: Bill Gardner,
　　Brian Miller

The "Bicycle Box" promotion opens to reveal
separate sheets with a consistent die cut edge. Each
piece has a large, clear photo of a bike part/tool
with a descriptive line relating in concept to the
picture.

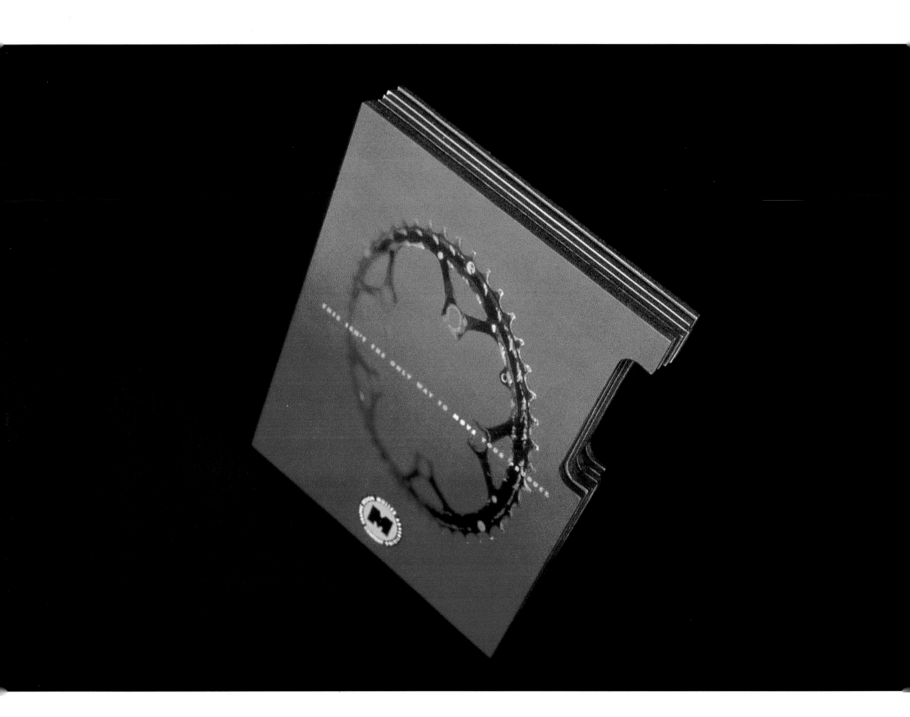

Creative Firm: Muller + Co.
  Kansas City, Missouri
Client: Muller + Co.
Business: Design firm
Art Director, Designer: Jeff Miller

"This tradeshow promotional series featured LPG at the Oklahoma Food Expo. An original-recipe salsa was conjured up for this occasion and packaged in jars to be handed out at the food expo. Jars were also promoted in the table top display. Promotional t-shirts with the salsa logo duplicated on them were handed out to sales people at the tradeshow. The western-themed show drew quite a crowd that seemed to enjoy the LPG salsa made especially for the occasion."

150

Creative Firm: Love Packaging Group
   Wichita, Kansas
Client: Love Packaging Group
Business: Packaging design studio
Creative: Rick Gimlin, Dustin Commer,
   Jack Jacobs

Game Show Network affiliate kit came in a box
with a TV screen cutout. Inside, material was
presented in true game-show fashion including
bright colors, and even a game spinner that
indicated what the user would "win."

Creative Firm: Lee Hunt Associates
   New York, New York
Client: Game Show Network
Business: Television network
Creative Directors: David Seeley, Cheri Dorr
Designer: Colleen Bothwell

152

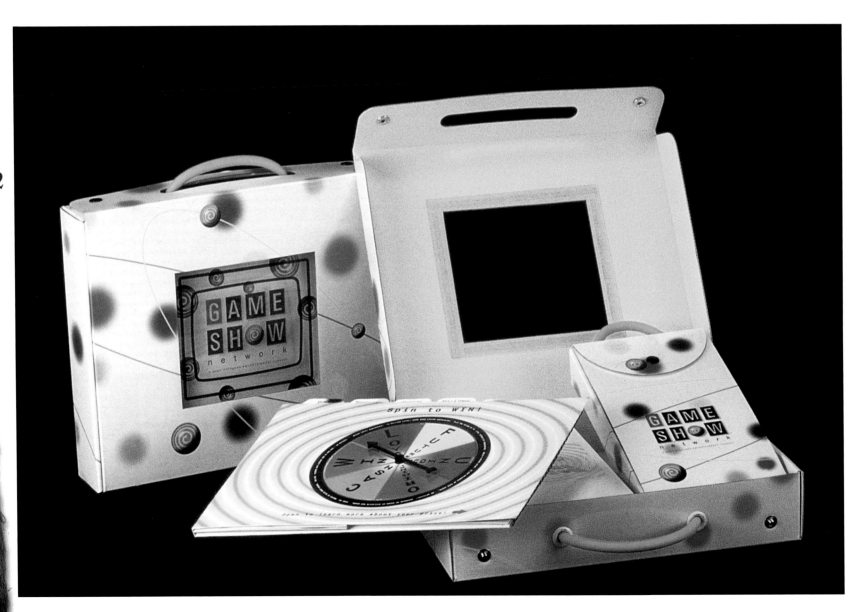

153

"To promote Turner Classic Movies Summer of Darkness Film Noir Festival, Banks Albers Design created a set of refrigerator magnets. The theme, 'A Recipe for Trouble,' already parodied how actual recipes are written, so the refrigerator magnets weren't that far of a stretch.

"Unique promotions like these have become a must for networks to stand out in the barrage of materials that are sent to cable operators. TCM uses a serious, but fun, approach for its business-to-business promotions By keeping the TCM name in front of cable operators longer than a typical 2D printed promotion, the magnets generated an interaction with the target audience reinforcing the TCM brand. Plus, they just looked cool."

Creative Firm: Banks Albers Design
    Atlanta, Georgia
Client: Turner Classic Movies
Business: Cable network/entertainment
Creative: Scott Banks, Kevin Fitzgerald

A myriad of uses for Rives paper is demonstrated in the contents of this paper box. Die cuts, pop-ups, and different printing techniques show the client the versatility of the stock.

Creative Firm: Design Club
   Tokyo, Japan
Client: Arjo Wiggins Fine Paper Ltd.
Business: Paper manufacturer
Art Director, Designer: Akihiko Tsukamoto
Illustrator: Yenpitsu Nemoto
Copywriter: Haruki Nagumo

Domino's Heatwave Kit, full of sales information,
is delivered in a newly-designed—what else?—
pizza box!

Creative Firm: Campbell Mithun Esty
  Minneapolis, Minnesota
Client: Domino's Pizza
Business: Pizza restaurant—delivery, takeout
Creative Directors: Barb Meeker,
  Jo-Anne Ebensteiner
Art Director: JC Estensen
Copywriter: Mary Lou Hidalgo

"Designed by student, Amy Fowler, as a means of promoting herself as a photographer's assistant, this unique promotion was contained in a kraft box. The box lid had an enticing line—'Please Don't…'. Inside the box, nested atop a spiral of raffia was a wire-bound book, 'Please Don't Shoot Me', which contained samples of her B&W photography and information about her skills."

Creative Firm: Tom Fowler, Inc.
   Stamford, Connecticut
Client: Amy Fowler
Business: Student
Creative: Amy Fowler

158

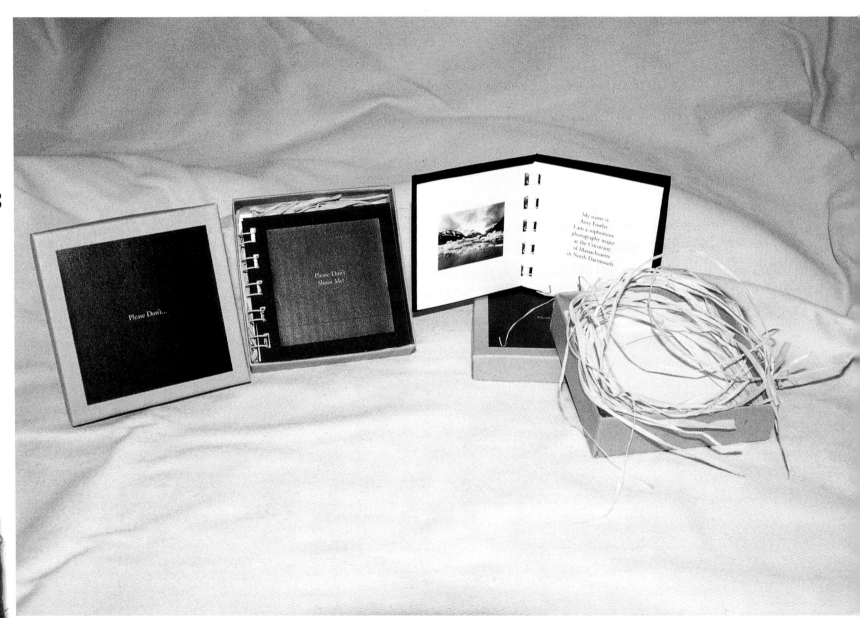

WE KNOW IT'S YOUR BIRTHDAY.

SPIRIT MOUNTAIN CASINO

HAPPY BIRTHDAY FROM YOUR FRIENDS AT SPIRIT MOUNTAIN CASINO.

SPIRIT MOUNTAIN CASINO

COYOTE CLUB
SPIRIT MOUNTAIN
CASINO

WE JUST THOUGHT IT BEST TO KEEP IT UNDER WRAPS.

159

"It was decided to utilize Spirit Mountain's existing database (which included the birth dates of high rollers) to motivate a return to the casino. No solicitation was made, but one week prior to the birthday, this gift was sent. The communication was meant only as a 'feel good' ('warm and fuzzy') gift to keep Spirit Mountain top of mind."

Creative Firm: Jack Nadel, Inc.
　Los Angeles, California
Client: Spirit Mountain Casino
Business: Upscale Native American gaming casino
Creative Director, Copywriter: Scott Brown

"This beautiful invitation, each created by hand, acted as an invitation and a promotion for Tom Fowler, Inc., which expressed our attention to detail and our elegant treatment of the graphics. This became an instant collector's item.

"Each invitation was created from a Japanese Saki box. The plexi-glass lid and Saki box were drilled by hand, and connected with red embroidery thread. The invitation inside was hand cut and inserted into the Saki box. As the recipient gently pulled out the invitation, it exposed the final information on a blue panel that created the sky."

161

Creative Firm: Tom Fowler, Inc.
  Stamford, Connecticut
Client: Tom Fowler, Inc.
Business: Graphic designers
Creative: Thomas G. Fowler

"Sex is fun. Some people think sex with condoms is not fun. To help change attitudes, a series of upbeat, tiny packages was created to hold condoms, instructions, and places to go if you have questions about safe(r) sex, AIDS, or STDs. The miniature packets are handed out at clubs, events, conferences, and health centers."

Creative Firm: After Hours Creative
  Phoenix, Arizona
Client: Phoenix Body Positive,
  Project Lifeguard and VIDA
Business: AIDS/HIV prevention
  and education
Creative: After Hours Creative

162

"These are DM cards for a small interior design company which works exclusively with fabrics. Pieces of fabric are attached to the cards."

Creative Firm:
  Sagmeister, Inc.
  New York, New York
Client: Fabrica
Business:
  Interior design
Art Director:
  Stefan Sagmeister
Designers:
  Stefan Sagmeister,
  Susanne Poelleritzer
Photographer:
  Michael Grimm

"GE Capital Assurance, a provider of annuities and insurance, was launching a program to attract the attention of a select group of brokerage general agencies (BGAs) and to introduce its financial services. In order to garner valuable BGA support, the company needed to create a unique and innovative marketing package that leveraged the well-established reputation of the company's ultimate parent, General Electric.

"The company had scheduled a presentation for this select group and wanted a breakthrough from traditional marketing materials to function as a creative hook to present at the meeting. This hook was to represent the company as the premium financial services provider and communicate a service-oriented, innovative personality.

"The resulting piece uses a tactile, three-dimensional approach. Presented to each BGA in a printed box, a silk-screened plexi-glass plate

164

165

introduces GE Capital Assurance's seven resources that allow the company to commit to providing a quality product. Centered in the piece is a clear acrylic cube that can be kept and used for a desk ornament or paper weight. Floating within the cube is a magic eye image with the GE logo, tying in the company's current advertising campaign.

The brochure surrounds the cube and incorporates an aluminum fastener binding, textured paper stocks, bold and colorful type treatments, and a creative application of embossing. These elements keep the recipient interested throughout the contextual information and call attention to the main selling points."

Creative Firm: Hornall Anderson Design Works
   Seattle, Washington
Client: GE Capital Assurance
Business: Annuities company
Art Director: John Hornall
Designers: John Hornall, Lisa Cerveny,
   Suzanne Haddon

The World Watch Promo came packaged in a round tin. The face of the watch had no numbers, but was printed with many geographic locations from around the world. The significance of the places is not clear at first sight, but an easy guess would be that these are where Supon offices are found.

Creative Firm: Supon Design Group, Inc.
  Washington, D.C.
Client: Supon Design Group, Inc.
Business: Design firm
Creative Director, Art Director:
  Supon Phornirunlit
Designer: Sharisse Steber

166

This firm's holiday invitation included a bottle of "seasoned greetings" with instructions on imbibing. The entire package used a combination of textures (shiny metal, glass, paper, and raffia) that might not always work together, but here creates a nice unity.

Creative Firm: NiCE Ltd.
   New York, New York
Client: NiCE Ltd.
Business: Design firm
Creative Director, Designer: Davide Nicosia

Multimedia kit was created to highlight Science Museum of Minnesota's "The Greatest Places" program. The Greatest Places are all locations of abounding natural beauty with which most Americans are not overly-familiar.

168

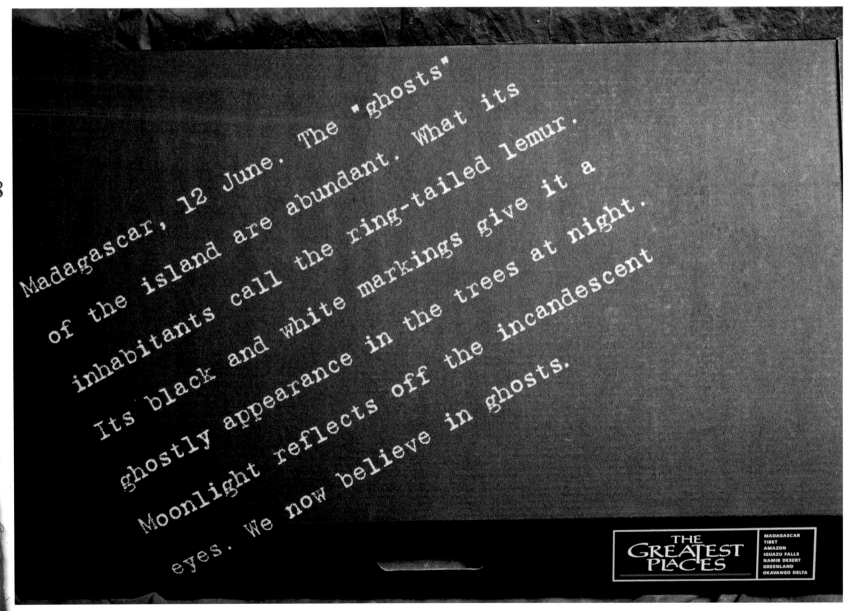

Madagascar, 12 June. The "ghosts" of the island are abundant. What its inhabitants call the ring-tailed lemur. Its black and white markings give it a ghostly appearance in the trees at night. Moonlight reflects off the incandescent eyes. We now believe in ghosts.

THE GREATEST PLACES

MADAGASCAR
TIBET
AMAZON
IGUAZU FALLS
NAMIB DESERT
GREENLAND
OKAVANGO DELTA

169

Creative Firm: Campbell Mithun Esty
 Minneapolis, Minnesota
Client: Science Museum of Minnesota
Business: Museum
Creative Directors: Jo-Anne Ebensteiner,
 Scott Webster
Art Director: Lisa Abrahamson
Copywriter: Joe Stefanson

"A suiter, with appropriate packaging, was selected to grab the recipients' attention and induce them to make the minimum number of calls to claim the gift. The packaging selected was a long, rectangular box with a funky suit illustration. The item was the most popular premium item the hotel has ever given. Calls made via AT&T Direct Service jumped during this period."

Creative Firm: Mega Pacific Graphic Design Inc.
  Pasig, Philippines
Client: AT&T Philippines
Business: Communication
Creative: Megpac

170

"We were asked to design a notebook for a creative conference in Bangkok titled 'Creasia'. Since the (existing) logo of the conference was an eye, we faxed to ALL participants, found out their eye color and had individual glass eyeballs manufactured to match. We put them in the die cut of the notebook. *Don't blink*.

"The notebook came in a box with compartments for all the xeroxed speeches."

Creative Firm: Leo Burnett Design Group
New York, New York
Client: Leo Burnett/Asia
Business: Creative conference
Art Director: Stefan Sagmeister
Designers: Stefan Sagmeister, Peter Rae,
Andrew Pogson, Mike Chan

"Different kinds of merchandise were used to promote Southgate."

Creative Firm: Emery Vincent Design
    Southbank, Australia
Client: Southgate
Business: Commerical property development
Creative: Emery Vincent Design team

"The Hornall Anderson Design Works online direct mail 'can' promo was designed to introduce potential clients and partners to HADW's work, capabilities, team, and design/development philosophy by guiding them to the firm's new website.

"The can mailing carries on from the initial 'bottle' mailing (page 108). A field can opener was included in the package to entice the recipient to open the can and learn more about Hornall Anderson's web and online capabilities."

Creative Firm: Hornall Anderson Design Works
  Seattle, Washington
Client: Hornall Anderson Design Works
Business: Graphic design firm
Art Director: Jack Anderson
Designers: Jack Anderson, Chris Sallquist,
  John Anicker, Mary Hesler, Shawn Sutherland,
  David Bates, Sonja Max

174

"In order to get a large attendance in the sales launch event, a silver metallic box with a teaser line on the lid was given away. Inside the box were puzzle pieces which the recipients needed to put together. When formed, it actually was a cryptic message which heightened the mystery even more. Within the puzzle was given the date, venue, and time where the mystery would finally be unraveled."

"The attendance was the biggest ever in comparison to the previous product launches."

Creative Firm: Mega Pacific Graphic Design, Inc.
   Pasig City, Philippines
Client: Citibank, N.A.
Business: Banking
Creative: Megpac

"My best friends, Tom and Tina, got married so I designed this invitation printed on silk and Japanese vellum paper. Instructions told you to place the silk on warm water and position the printed wedding couple (on the vellum) on the piece of silk. The couple started to literally dance on silk. And that's what marriage is all about."

Creative Firm:
  Sagmeister, Inc.
  New York, New York
Client: Tom & Tina
  Schierlitz/Budewig
Business: Private
Art Director, Designer:
  Stefan Sagmeister

"Every year, Aspen Traders, a retailer of clothing, jewelry, home furnishings, and body products, sends a Christmas card to its customers. The card has to be a nondenominational seasonal celebration due to the diversity of Aspen Trader's customer list. A goal set forth by the owner was that the card draw influence from a current fashion trend toward patterns that have their roots in tribal and regional tattoos. After much struggle with trying to merge the holiday with tattoo influences from around the world, we developed this set of reaching hands, grasping a star. The tattoo-influenced pattern covering the hands is very reminiscent of Moroccan tattoos which is appropriate since Aspen Traders carries clothing and jewelry with a very 'worldly' feel.

"Every year, we produce a three-dimensional card for Aspen Traders with the challenge that it must easily assemble and fold down flat for mailing. This year was no exception—the star 'notches in' on the thumb and finger of the tallest hand and the whole piece is then accordion-folded flat to be inserted into envelopes. Another challenge is that the owners like to include the names of all the employees on the card. We always try to work them subtly into the design, so this year we worked the names into the tattoo pattern on the back side of the card. The card was very successful and received a great response from clients who really appreciated receiving such a custom card, making them feel appreciated in turn."

Creative Firm: Gardner Design
     Wichita, Kansas
Client: Aspen Traders
Business: Clothing, jewelry, home
     furnishings, etc. retail store
Art Director: Bill Gardner
Designers: Bill Gardner, Brian Miller

178

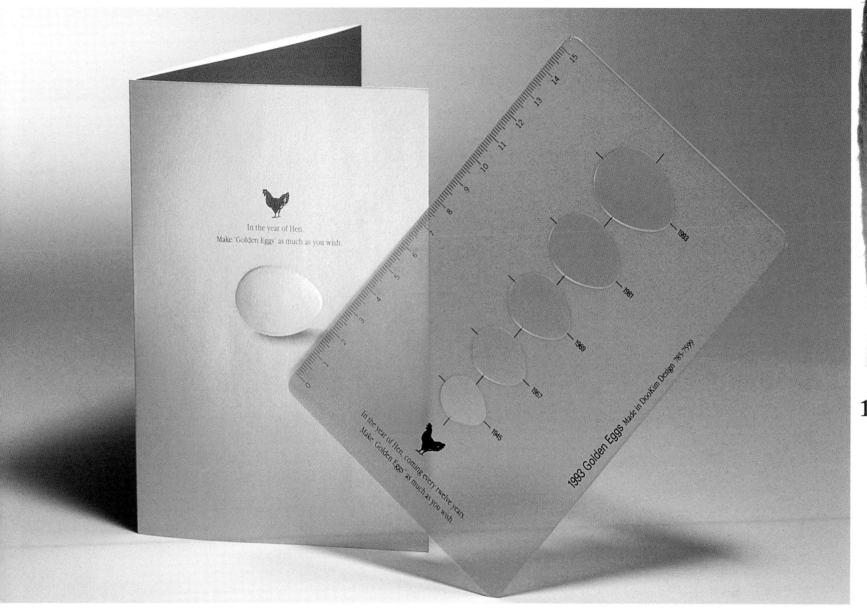

In the year of Hen.
Make 'Golden Eggs' as much as you wish.

In the year of Hen, coming every twelve years.
Make 'Golden Eggs' as much as you wish.

1993 Golden Eggs. Made in DooKim Design 785-7599

"As one of the designer's favorite tools, this greeting card was presented in the shape and form of a template in recognition of 1993, the Year of the Hen. It presented the Golden Egg in template form and invited everyone to 'Make Golden Eggs as much as you wish.'"

Creative Firm: DooKim Inc.
    Seoul, Korea
Client: DooKim Inc.
Business: Design company
Creative: Doo Kim

"This unique promotion consisted of a carrier folder and several inserts. The objective was to create a piece that demonstrated the ability of King James Cast Coat paper to be printed, scored, and folded without a cracked edge. We created a piece that allowed the paper specifier to actually fold the printed stock to demonstrate this unique and sought-after capability.

180

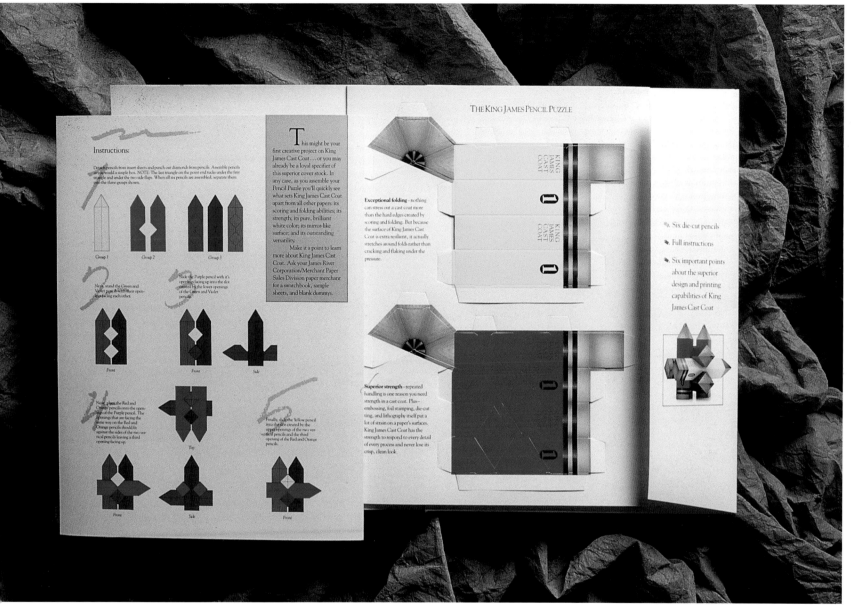

THE KING JAMES PENCIL PUZZLE

Instructions:

Detach pencil from insert sheets and punch out diamonds from pencils. Assemble pencils as you would a simple box. NOTE: The last triangle on the point end tucks under the first triangle and under the two side flaps. When all six pencils are assembled, separate them into the three groups shown.

Group 1   Group 2   Group 3

Next, stand the Green and Violet pencils with their openings facing each other.

Slide the Purple pencil with it's openings facing up into the slot created by the lower openings of the Green and Violet pencils.

Front   Front   Side

Next, place the Red and Orange pencils onto the openings of the Purple pencil. The openings that are facing the same way on the Red and Orange pencils should fit against the sides of the two vertical pencils leaving a third opening facing up.

Finally, slide the Yellow pencil into the slot created by the upper openings of the two vertical pencils and the third opening of the Red and Orange pencils.

Front   Top   Front

Front   Side   Front

This might be your first creative project on King James Cast Coat . . . or you may already be a loyal specifier of this superior cover stock. In any case, as you assemble your Pencil Puzzle you'll quickly see what sets King James Cast Coat apart from all other papers: its scoring and folding abilities; its strength; its pure, brilliant white color; its mirror-like surface; and its outstanding versatility.

Make it a point to learn more about King James Cast Coat. Ask your James River Corporation/Merchant Paper Sales Division paper merchant for a swatchbook, sample sheets, and blank dummies.

Exceptional folding - nothing can stress out a cast coat more than the hard edges created by scoring and folding. But because the surface of King James Cast Coat is extra resilient, it actually stretches around folds rather than cracking and flaking under pressure.

Superior strength—repeated handling is one reason you need strength in a cast coat. Plus—embossing, foil stamping, die-cutting, and lithography itself put a lot of strain on a paper's surfaces. King James Cast Coat has the strength to respond to every detail of every process and never lose its crisp, clean look.

KING JAMES CAST COAT

- Six die-cut pencils
- Full instructions
- Six important points about the superior design and printing capabilities of King James Cast Coat

"The cover of the folder showed a photograph of the pencil puzzle fully assembled. Inside the folder, one insert instructed how to assemble the puzzle. There were three inserts printed, scored, and die cut which were used to create the pencils that actually made the puzzle."

Creative Firm: Tom Fowler, Inc. Stamford, Connecticut
Client: James River Corporation
Business: Paper manufacturer
Creative: Thomas G. Fowler, Karl Maruyama, Elizabeth P. Ball

"The panoramic photos determined this calendar's horizontal format. The bottom are the twelve months of the year, with the current month enlarged. The nature photos are enhanced with six-color hexachrome, and underprinted with metallic inks to add an extra glow. To deliver this oversize calendar, a coordinated litho-printed corrugate box was created."

Creative Firm: Belyea
Client: K/P
Business: Printing company
Art Director: Patricia Belyea
Designer: Ron Lars Hansen
Photographer: Pete Saloutos

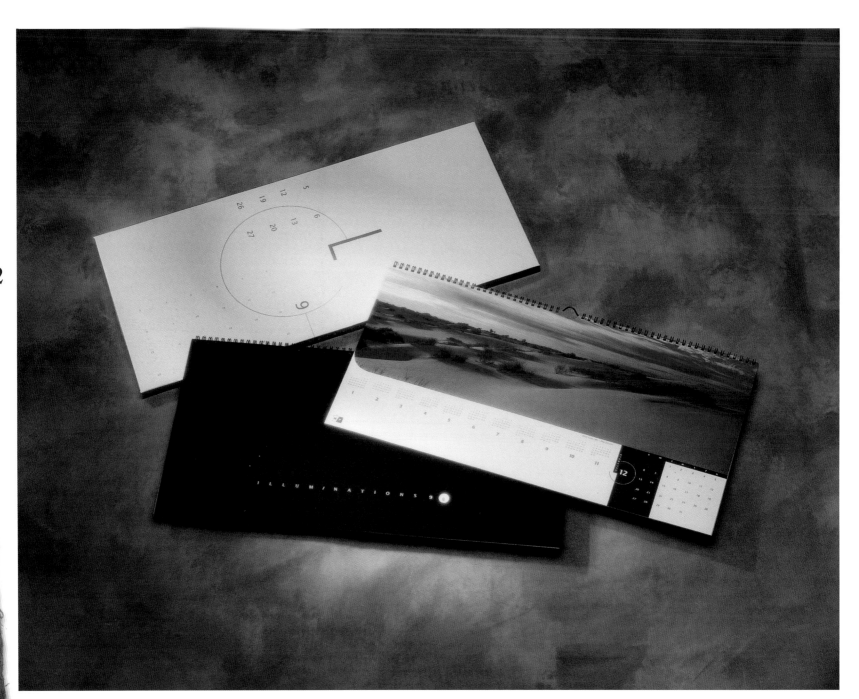

"The Wilkins family has a unique occurrence every year. Three generations of Wilkins men (the Howards) all share the same birthday, and they're all 30 years apart in age. So, when they turned 30, 60, and 90, the family wanted to throw a huge bash. They knew their invitation had to be beyond the ordinary. The theme of a tree/log with rings representing years was chosen, and we knew we needed to send an actual log to make the invite stand out. We worked with a saw mill to come up with slabs of oak log that were just the right thickness. Then we came up with a laser cut design for the top of the log and a coating that helped prevent the log slab from splitting. The only thing left was the design of the circular booklet which was screwed onto the top of the log. We dedicated a page to each Howard, and used the tree ring pattern in the background to highlight unusual events that occurred over the years during each Howard's lifetime.

"The invitations packed the party and several other job opportunities arose when recipients inquired about the design firm that produced them."

Creative Firm: Gardner Design
  Wichita, Kansas
Client: The Wilkins Family
Art Directors, Designers: Bill Gardner,
  Brian Miller

INDEX

184